Richard Grant White

National Hymns

How they are Written and how they are not Written

Richard Grant White

National Hymns
How they are Written and how they are not Written

ISBN/EAN: 9783744784290

Printed in Europe, USA, Canada, Australia, Japan

Cover: Foto ©Thomas Meinert / pixelio.de

More available books at **www.hansebooks.com**

NATIONAL HYMNS.

HOW THEY ARE WRITTEN AND HOW THEY ARE NOT WRITTEN

A LYRIC AND NATIONAL STUDY FOR THE TIMES

By
RICHARD GRANT WHITE

NEW YORK:
RUDD & CARLETON, 130 GRAND STREET
AND
GEORGE W. ELLIOTT, 89 WALKER STREET.
M DCCC LXI.

Entered, according to Act of Congress, in the year 1861, by
RUDD & CARLETON,
In the Clerk's Office of the District Court of the United States for the Southern District of New York.

R. CRAIGHEAD,
Printer, Stereotyper, and Electrotyper,
Carton Building,
81, 83, and 85 Centre Street.

To

MOSES H. GRINNELL,

THIS SLIGHT TOKEN

OF ADMIRATION OF HIS ABILITIES, OF HONOR FOR HIS PATRIOTISM,

AND OF HIGH PERSONAL REGARD.

The Committee upon a National Hymn placed some of the "most meritorious" and otherwise "noticeable" songs received by them in the hands of Messrs. Rudd & Carleton for publication under my editorial care. There were very few of these—not thirty, all told; and those which were remarkable for lyric excellence were gradually so reduced in numbers by the withdrawal of manuscripts by their authors, that after a while the original project was abandoned.

Of all the motives which may have induced a withdrawal of consent to publication, or a withholding of it where it was reasonably expected, it is not necessary, or, indeed, proper, here to speak. Upon such a point every author has not only the right of deciding for himself, but of doing so unquestioned. It is proper, however, to say that in some instances consent to publication was refused owing to the disposition shown by many competitors to make themselves disagreeable, and to say as many unpleasant things as their ingenuity could devise about the committee and its doings. As some, though by no means all, of the best songs were written by authors of reputation, it was natural that a part of these, at least, should shrink from exposure to the threatened consequences. One of them remarked, "If I were at the beginning of my career, I should not mind such talk; but as it is plain that everything ill-natured that can be said is to be said, I had rather not put myself into such a pillory." It is right also to add that this pitiful conduct was exhibited invariably by those competitors who had no claim whatever to special consideration. Certain of the hymns which would otherwise have been published were withdrawn by their authors in a very courteous and good-natured manner; but the people who talked and fumed, who wearied the members of the committee with calls and letters of remonstrance and inquiry, who waylaid them in the streets, who entered the office of the publishers big with bombast and terrible with threats—some, if their verses were published, some, if they were not—were invariably those whose manuscripts had fallen on the first reading dead into the waste basket, leaving not even a trace behind them in the memory to aid a guess at what their incensed authors were raving about.

But although the notion of publishing the projected volume was therefore given up, it was afterwards thought by some of those who had been interested in the undertaking that some discussion of the subject of national hymns, with an account of the origin and proceedings of the committee in question, illustrated by songs selected in part from those which had been left at the disposal of the committee would be acceptable to many persons; and therefore I have given a few days to the preparation of this little book. For it I only am responsible. I have not the right, had I the desire, to claim the support of any of my colleagues for a single opinion set forth in it. In scope, it has falsified the Horatian warning as to the unexpected issue of the turning wheel. I undertook only a few pages of introductory remarks and narrative; but my work grew under my hand, and the result, though still a trifle, is something more, as well as something other, than that which I sat down to write. If many of my readers find in the little book only what they had already learned, I shall be pleased that I address so well-informed a circle; and let them be thankful that they know so much more than their neighbors. If any intelligent reader disapproves of what is here written, he will owe me something for having furnished him with a topic of elegant social discussion with some other more intelligent reader who approves. The more animated and general the dispute, the better for the publishers, who have invested money in paper which might have made cartridges, and type which might have done service as bullets.

I have some friends in England, and more in America, who know the deep and abiding love and reverence I have for all that is good, and great, and honorable in English character, in English history and letters—and there is so much of it—and how I prize my English birthright. These may wonder at some passages in this little volume, until they reflect a moment upon the very obvious fact, that those passages do not touch upon what I regard as lovely and venerable in the English character, or—as I am at once glad and sorry to say—as essentially English at all. So, too, I have friends among my Southern fellow-citizens who know that although I believe, with some Southern statesmen, whose names are favorably known to the world, that slavery is a wrong and an evil, I am neither Abolitionist nor "Black" Republican; and whom, if they are surprised at anything I have written, I would remind that what the men who control the South are now fighting for is something that has never brought honor to any nation, and which has been long the reproach of this country throughout civilized Christendom. Reproach which we who were in no sense justly open to it have yet borne for the sake of brotherhood, and the ultimate benefit of our country and the world; and which we are willing still to bear, so long as they who inflict the wrong and hug the evil, do not insist upon our sharing their fearful responsibility.

This, however, not by way of apology, or even deprecation. I have not one word to take back or to regret. But I do ask the reader's pardon for detaining him so long here, while, like an over-anxious host, I press upon him half my entertainment at the threshold.

R. G. W.

NEW YORK, *Sept.* 16*th*, 1861.

NATIONAL HYMNS.

I.

In the Spring of the present year a new want began to be felt in this country. The batteries with which the faithful commander of Fort Sumter had, with silent guns, seen himself surrounded during four long months, opened fire upon the national flag floating from a military post of the United States, and he and his handful of brave soldiers were burned out of the strong-hold from which it does not appear that they could have otherwise been driven. Indignation flashed through the astonished land; and the loyal citizens of the Republic rose as one man to avenge the wrong and defend the national existence. The whole country quivered with a new emotion. Men lived in the open air that they might read in each other's faces, eye to eye, the noble wrath, the fixed determination, the lofty purpose that ruled the hour. Two could hardly speak together in the street above their ordinary tone without being surrounded by eager listeners. Every public place was thronged by unbidden crowds, intent upon the discussion of the momentous situation; and more formal meetings, numbering from hundreds to tens of thousands, were common. A nation of freemen, each one of whom felt, at last, his own responsibility for his country's safety and honor, was pierced through brain and heart with the barbed conviction that that safety was in peril, and that honor was at stake.

Party barriers fell as if by magic; and we all found ourselves side by side with one feeling, one purpose, forgetful of the past, absorbed in the present and the future. Patriotism, which had been trodden under the feet of politicians, which had withered in the arid soil of selfishness under the blazing sun of prosperity, which had been choked with the thorns of care, and wealth, and pleasure, struck at once its roots to the very centre of the nation's being, and in a single night blossomed into fruitfulness. That fruit was a stern resolution to sacrifice life and fortune in defence of the republic. But stern although it was, there was mixed with it no hatred, no vindictiveness.* The insurgents were enemies only in so far

* "I have nowhere in the North," said the late Secretary of War, Mr. Holt of Kentucky, in his New York speech of September 3rd, 'found any feeling of exasperation against the people of the South."

as they were enemies of the republic for which their fathers and ours had toiled, and fought, and died together. The resentment was pure of all personality, and consistent with all charity and individual good will. Nay, it was mingled with sorrow and pity for men and brethren, whose judgment had been so blinded, and whose moral sense had been so perverted by the holding of an inferior race in slavery, as to enable trading politicians, disappointed or fearing disappointment, to prepare them for, and finally lead them into a rebellion against, what one of themselves has well styled, " the most beneficent government the world ever saw:" a rebellion, unsupported even by the slightest prospective danger to slavery wherever it was made locally secure by the organic compact of the nation, but having for its sole motive the determination, either to make the interest of slavery dominant in this country, and to pervert the flag of this free republic to the protection of inchoate slave communities, or to rend and ruin the great nation in which that interest had ceased to rule.

This purpose was regarded as a wicked one; but it was the sin that was hated, not the sinners; and, to illustrate this period by glancing forward from it—if the national forces, instead of succumbing to their humiliating and causeless panic at Manassas Junction, had been able to follow up and complete their first well won success, there would have been joy, indeed, throughout the loyal States; but no exultation, no triumph, no festivities, no illuminations would have celebrated that victory. Government would have but performed one of its gravest functions; loyal citizens would have but absolved themselves of one of their highest duties; deserving therefore, however, none the less, the gratitude of their country than if they had protected its interests, its honor, or even its existence against a foreign foe. The feeling thus awakened, though so considerate and so placable, was yet enthusiastic. The fire of patriotism never burned with purer, brighter, or intenser flame, than in the breasts of the Americans who were so startled by the guns of Sumter.

Such was the feeling of the hour; and with such emotions glowing in their breasts, men met continually in greater or smaller assemblages, where, alternately relieved and excited by each other's eloquence—for then the simplest utterance of patriotism seemed eloquent—there was yet one want most sorely felt. A national hymn was lacking. The strong feeling of great numbers always tends to utterance in song. Music is the universal language of emotion. It is that in which, with rare exceptions, all can give vent to excitement, that without it must be repressed. Men will sing what they would be shamefaced to say. Music has the twofold effect of stimulating and relieving the grand passions of the soul.

But no little of its power in awakening sentiment and keeping it alive, is derived from its association with words or with events. There was no particular æsthetic reason why the brave, calm English soldiers should sing "Annie Laurie" in their cheerless camp before Sevastopol, and weep while they sang or listened. There are other ballads just as sweet as that sweet ballad, as there are other girls as dear as Annie Laurie; but it happened to be a favorite in England when the war broke out; it mingled with the memories of fading Dover cliffs, and told those tearful, bearded heroes of the girls they had left behind them. The Swiss herdsmen's songs are beautiful; but the songs that Mozart wrote are far more beautiful, with a beauty higher, tenderer, more essential, more enduring. Yet the strains of the herdsman never die out of a Switzer's ear, and ever call him back to his mountain home with sad imperiousness, while he is content to admire Mozart wherever he can hear him to the best advantage. It is not safe to measure the power of music by the effects that it produces, or to trust to the genuineness of feeling exhibited under its influence. So many dull ears and honest hearts think that they are enjoying music when they are only resting their heads once more in their mothers' laps, or trembling again with the sweet tumults of their first passion; so many sensitive organizations think that they are wrapt in the fervor of religious worship, when they are but spell-bound by the enchanting strains of Haydn or of Cherubini.

Music affords a pleasure neither purely intellectual nor purely sensual. More than any other art, more than any other means of impressing the human organization, it addresses itself to man's entire nature. With those who really feel its power, it takes mind and soul, and sense all captive. It does not refine;

it does not elevate; it does not strengthen. It leaves the moral nature quite untouched. It has no moral, nay, no intellectual influence whatever. Pages of weak sentiment and fallacious speculation have been written upon the contrary assumption; volumes of nonsense have been talked and retalked, in ever diluting and re-diluting feebleness. Some of the greatest scoundrels that ever lived, some of the feeblest intellects, some of the most grovelling souls, have possessed not only the finest and most sensitive musical organizations, but the most exquisite musical taste; have thrilled themselves, and have sent responsive thrills through throngs of cultivated hearers by the mere spell of their own voices. Where are there pettier jealousies or fiercer hates than among musicians?—private or public, it makes no difference. Not by reason of their art, but altogether in spite of it. It does absolutely nothing towards the elevation of intellectual tone, or the mitigation of moral deformity. Let any man ask himself if he ever spoke the more kindly to a shivering beggar, or was tenderer of the feelings of a friend because he had just turned his back upon the opera-house and was still palpitating with the exquisite pleasure of hearing Alboni's *Ah non credea*. We are told that the angels sing in heaven; but were not the Sirens monsters from below the lungs? and do men need to lash themselves to masts to keep from rushing heavenward? Sometimes it seems as if the Poets were wiser than the Apostles.

But Music, we know not why, is both a relief and

a stimulus to all emotion. It originates no sentiment, it develops none; but it quickens and subtilizes the action of all that are in being. It is not food for the soul, but wine. So with national music: patriotism must exist before patriotic songs are written. No man was ever brought to love his country by the music to which his countrymen sang their devotion. But if that heroic sentiment does dwell within his breast, either he is exceptional among his kind, or his country in its fortunes, if there do not arrive occasions when his whole soul yearns for musical expression. Patriotic feeling, like all other feeling excited by any unusual incident, seeks utterance in verse and music; and thus a national hymn seems almost as indispensable an appanage of nationality as a national flag. One of the first indications of an incipient revolution in France is the singing of the Marseillaise Hymn; and one of the first steps taken to restrain the outbreak is the suppression of the song. Only a few months ago the Poles, charged and fired upon by the Russian troops, as they assembled to present a petition in Warsaw, fell upon their knees, and sang their national hymn; thus fortifying themselves to endure an attack which they were powerless to repel.

And so when loyal Americans assembled in those dark days of the Republic which immediately followed the bombardment of Fort Sumter, they longed to sing; but there was no song suited to them or to the occasion. "The Star-Spangled Banner" had been growing in favor in the loyal States from the beginning of the secession movement, and was played continually by all military and orchestral bands, and sung often at concerts and private musical gatherings. But as a patriotic song for the people at large, as the National Hymn, it was found to be almost useless. The range of the air, an octave and a half, places it out of the compass of ordinary voices; and no change that has been made in it has succeeded in obviating this paramount objection, without depriving the music of that characteristic spirit which is given by its quick ascent through such an extended range of notes.

The words, too, are altogether unfitted for a national hymn. They are almost entirely descriptive, and of a particular event. Such lines as these have not a sufficiently general application for a national hymn; they paint a picture, they do not embody a sentiment:—

"On the shore dimly seen through the mists of the deep,
    Where the foe's haughty host in dread silence reposes,
What is that which the breeze o'er the towering steep
    As it fitfully blows, half conceals, half discloses?
Now it catches the gleam of the morning's first beam,
In full glory reflected, now shines on the stream."

The lines are, also, too long, and the rhyme too involved for a truly popular patriotic song. They tax the memory: they should aid it. The rhythm, too, is complicated, and often harsh and vague.

"Oh! thus be it ever when free men shall stand
    Between their loved home, and the war's desolation;
Blest with victory and peace, may the Heaven-rescued land
    Praise the power that hath made and preserved us a nation."

In fact, only the choral lines of this song have brought it into general favor.

"And the Star-Spangled Banner in triumph shall wave
O'er the land of the free and the home of the brave."

But even in regard to this, who cannot but wish that the spangles could be taken out, and a good, honest flag be substituted for the banner!

"The Star-Spangled Banner," though for these reasons so utterly inadequate to the requirements of a national hymn that the people stood mute while in some instances it was sung by a single voice, or in most cases it was only played by a band, is yet far the best of the three songs which, for lack of better, have until now been called American national airs. Of the other two, Yankee Doodle has the claim of long association, and will probably always retain a certain degree of a certain kind of favor. But no sane person would ever dream of regarding it as a national hymn. Its words, as all know who have ever heard them, are mere childish burlesque; and its air, if air it must be called, is as comical as its words, and can hardly be regarded as being properly music. To set serious or even earnest words to this grotesque tune, would be only to excite laughter by absurd incongruity. It has been attempted; and the best result appears in the following spirited verses, in which the author of "The New Priest at Conception Bay" commemorated the encounter of the Sixth Massachusetts regiment with thé secession mob in Baltimore, on the anniversary of the skirmish at Lexington, April 19th, 1775.

THE MASSACHUSETTS LINE.

AIR: "*Yankee Doodle.*"

I.

Still first, as long and long ago,
   Let Massachusetts muster;
Give her the post right next the foe;
   Be sure that you may trust her.
She was the first to give her blood
   For freedom and for honor;
She trod her soil to crimson mud:
   God's blessing be upon her!

II.

She never faltered for the right,
   Nor ever will hereafter;
Fling up her name with all your might,
   Shake roof-tree and shake rafter.
But of old deeds she need not brag,
   How she broke sword and fetter;
Fling out again the old striped flag!
   She'll do yet more and better.

III.

In peace her sails fleck all the seas,
   Her mills shake every river;
And where are scenes so fair as these
   God and her true hands give her?
Her claim in war who seek to rob?
   All others come in later—
Her's first it is to front the Mob,
   The Tyrant and the Traitor.

IV.

God bless, God bless the glorious State!
  Let her have her way to battle!
She'll go where batteries crash with fate,
  Or where thick rifles rattle.
Give her the Right, and let her try,
  And then, who can, may press her;
She'll go straight on, or she will die;
  God bless her! and God bless her!

DUANESBURGH, May 7, 1861.

Excellent this, and all the better because it is true, which cannot be said of the greater number of national lyrics. But attempt to sing it to the air to the rhythm of which it is written, and you will not be able to finish the first stanza for laughing. To intone the benediction at the end of the first and last stanzas to the notes of the last phrase of the air, would put the gravity of the Reverend writer to a test which not all his sense of professional decorum would enable him to sustain. And so although we must partly admit the truth of the following lines from one of the proposed National Hymns, sent to the New York Committee,

"Familiar too as household name,
  Is Yankee Doodle's thrilling song;
It cheers the warrior in the field,
  It triumphs in the festive throng;"

we must yet confess that the "thrilling song" in question hardly meets the requirements of the present state of civilization.

"Hail Columbia" is really worse than "Yankee

Doodle." **That has** a character, although it is comic; and it is respectable, because it makes no pretence. But both the words and music of "Hail Columbia" are common-place, vulgar, and pretentious; **and** the people themselves have found all this out.*

* The "Star-Spangled **Banner**" **is an old** French air, long known in **England as** " Anacreon **in Heaven," and in America as** " Adams **and Liberty," until the** song so designated was supplanted by Key's. The air **to which** Hopkinson wrote "Hail Columbia" was **a** march written by a German band-master on **occasion of** a visit of Washington, when President, to the old John street theatre in New York. It was called the "President's March." Yankee Doodle is an old English air.

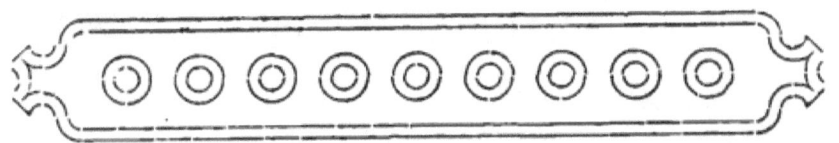

II.

And so we are practically without a national hymn. That we have thus far remained so, must be attributed in part to the brevity of our national existence, partly to the peaceful and prosperous course of that existence, until now—for national peril, or, at least, national triumph, is needful to the strong development of the sentiment of nationality—and partly to the fact that it is only of late years that music, excepting psalmody, has been cultivated by all sorts and conditions of men among us.

For music is not a spontaneous product of the English race; and we are but Englishmen under new skies and new circumstances. The emigration from other races that has reached these shores, is, to all intents and purposes, as nothing. Comparatively very small, it is at once swallowed up, and becomes an undistinguishable part of the native element. By intermarriage, and yet more by dominant influence, in a generation or two, Irishmen, Germans, and

Frenchmen become Americans, their origin detected only by their names; and an American is but an Englishman, reared in a somewhat unkempt, unfinished republic, where work, and land, and social honor, and political distinction, are to be had by all men who will strive for them. This makes some difference between the British subject and the American citizen; but it is a difference of development, not of essential traits. Were the latter, from his childhood up, under as constant and severe a restraint as the former is, were failure in business, in profession, as ruinous here as it is in the mother country, Americans would cease to be independent, rash, and adventurous, and become submissive, cautious, and steady-going. Their so-called excitability (which is not excitability but mere mobility; for they are, if there be a difference, less excitable than their brothers across the water)* would give place to that steadiness of habit

---

* Thus, for instance, I remember having seen three first-rate ships, one of them a frigate, launched. The throngs which shared the sight were immense; people having come for miles, and stood hours waiting in the sun, for the sake of this almost momentary spectacle. In each case the launch was splendid; yet not a cheer went up. In what other country in the world would this have happened! Fanny Kemble, too, grumbles in her Journal that the audiences were sluggish, and that the pit did not rise to her father. Mrs. Charles Kean, and some of the great singers, have also complained of the coldness of the immense audiences which gathered to hear them, which yet gave every other proof of intelligent enjoyment, except excitement. Americans generally look and listen in silence. Their readiness for a new "sensation" is due in a great measure to their craving for novelty, and their freedom from those restraints which silently, but inexorably, check the movements of other nations.

which has been ascribed to a phlegmatic disposition. Thus the principal difference between the two branches into which the English stock has divided, would disappear. The Englishman has improved in America in some points, deteriorated in others; but the improvement concerns the many, the deterioration, the few. So, as a whole, the race has gained.

But the English traits, which are so well preserved in this country, are not those which are most remarked by people of other races in the England of to-day; but those which characterized us before the middle of the century 1600. For your British Englishman differs far more than your American Englishman from their common ancestor of only two hundred years ago. Differs more in person, in speech, in habit, in mind. John Bull is a creature of the last century. Before the reign of Anne no trace of him is to be found in history. The least gracious part of his character, that with which he seems to take a malicious pleasure in hiding his real worth, and his essential goodness and manliness of heart, and with which he is reproached by all nations, is a new development. Arrogant, supercilious, egotistical, selfish men there are in all nations; but no people, surely not the English, was ever accused by all the world of being made up chiefly of such men, until John Bull appeared. His very physiognomy is new. Look at the far-stretching galleries of well authenticated portraits of Englishmen, by painters of more or less eminence, from the time when portrait-painting was practised until 1650, and you will see that if John

Bull were in England then, he was not in the habit of sitting for his picture. And do not smile at the term American Englishman; for the Englishman has not his name because he was born in England; but England was called England because the English race dwelt there. The name goes with the people. The first England was a small patch of ground south of the Baltic sea; the next was the larger and the fairer part of the white-cliffed isle; the new England lies between the two great oceans.

In one respect at least, we faithfully preserve a distinctive trait of our race. We have no national music. In this deficiency, the English are peculiar among all the people of the earth. There is no national English music; we brought none over here with us, and we have originated none since we left the old home. There are songs, indeed, which are called English ballads; and there are certain very correctly written glees, mostly dolorous in their character; and also, English church "services" or sacred music, by which, such words as "We praise thee" and "O, be joyful," can be sung in a sufficiently penitential manner. But all this has no distinctive character, except it be that character which forbids it to be called music by any other civilized people, or to be listened to with patience by those among ourselves who happen to have musical organizations and cultivated taste. It is true, that certain composers, on both sides of the water, have produced some fine music—a very little; but its character has plainly shown that it was merely the isolated upspringing of

German, Italian, or French seeds, cultivated in English soil. We have no school of music; nay, we have not even a good popular air that is of our own production. The very commonest ballads which have been long in favor, both in England and America, are not of English origin; they are Scotch or Irish, French or Italian. Of "Home, Sweet Home" itself, the sentiment of the words—written by an American—is truly English, but the melody is Italian. And the very "Annie Laurie," which was sung so much in the Crimea, is Scotch.

This lack of popular English melodies has been before remarked. Tom Moore, in the Preface to his "Popular National Airs," says:—"It is Cicero, I believe, who says '*naturâ ad modos ducimur*,' and the abundance of wild, indigenous airs which almost every country, except England, possesses, sufficiently proves the truth of this assertion." This is true beyond denial. Among all other people, music cheers the toil of the husbandman; but no song goes up from fields tilled by the English race. We go to our work more seriously; nay, do we not, on whichever side of the Atlantic, keep up our wont of "taking our pleasure sadly," as a shrewd observer said we did four hundred years and more ago? It is not easy for us to break forth into song, whether at work or play, in peace or war. Taillefer, the Norman, who led the first charge upon the Englishmen at the battle of Hastings, singing *Chanson de Roland* as he rode, only got killed for his pains in attempting to force this outlandish fashion upon us at the sword's point, a fate which has deterred any one from following his example.* As for his race, they beat us in that fight; but we had our revenge in swallowing up our victors. In spite of his lance and his coat of mail, the Norman soon disappeared from the soil of England. And now we go to battle in the same impassible silent way in which our ancestors went before us. **Nay, when the Garibaldi Legion marched down Broadway to the**

---

* **An absurd** practice has so long obtained, of calling the two parties to the battle of Hastings, Normans and Saxons, and of dividing the nation ruled by the conquerors into two people, distinguished by the same names, for two hundred and fifty years after, that the designation of the latter as Englishmen may excite some surprise. But England was called England more than a thousand years ago, by its own inhabitants, and by those of neighboring countries, because English men, so calling themselves, and so called by others, inhabited it. The Normans fought Englishmen at Hastings, not Saxons. See this passage quoted by Percy from the *Roman de Vacce*, referring to the very incident above mentioned at that battle:—

> "Quant ils virent Normanz venir
> Mout reissiez *Engleiz* fremir, * * *
> **Taillefer qui mout bien chantoit,**
> Sur un cheval, qui tost alloit
> Devant euls aloit chantant
> De Kallemaigne, et de Rollant,
> **Et d'Ollivier** de Vassaux,
> Qui moururent en Raincesvaux."

See also these lines from Wace's *Roman de Rou*, written about 1140–50. The old romances are full of like evidence.

> "Des *Engleis* furent rei toz treis,
> **E toz treis** furent dus è reis
> Reis de *Engleterre* par cunquie,
> Et dus fure de Normendie."

war, with green sprigs in their hats, twirling their rifles in the air, and singing as they marched, did we not, while admiring, still feel a little shamefaced for them, as if they were guilty of some indecorum? which, nevertheless, after the assuming habit of our race, we graciously forgave them, because they were foreigners, and so did not know how to behave themselves "respectably."

It is beyond denial that there is no really English music, indigenous, "native and to the manner born," either in England or America. Of airs properly national, it should be remembered, the composers are not known. They are found existing among the people, who are ignorant of their origin. They are, to borrow a German phrase, folk-music.

This barrenness of popular melody is a reproach to us among the nations; and instead of admitting it candidly, we painfully go about to remove or evade it. On the other side of the water musical antiquaries gather together such faded and forlorn fag-ends of melody as they can find songs tacked to, and thus succeed only in establishing by auricular demonstration that we have been utterly unable to produce a popular air worth listening to.* Or they magnify the "solid and manly" style of Fairfax, Taverner, Shepherd, Bird, and all the other worthies so lauded and

---

* See, for instance, Chappell's "Collection of National English Airs," London, 1838; a work very creditable to the research of its author, but in which there is hardly an air more than a hundred and fifty years old, the frequent repetition of which would not make any real lover of music, except a Briton brimfull of prejudice, insane.

glorified by Master **Thomas Morley** in the dreary dialogues of " Practicall **Musicke**" which he holds with Polymathes and **Philomathes**, and which Humfrey Lownes imprinted for him at London in 1608. Or they sanctify **themselves** in the ecclesiastical style of Tallis and Boyce, Locke and Blow, on hearing or reading whose "learned" compositions, we wonder whether they were written by single or double entry, or were worked out upon the binomial theorem.*

In this country some of us being asked for our national melodies, reply, it seems, by referring our querists to the negro melodies !† They might as well fasten upon us the songs of the Chinese coolies in California, or the war-whoops of the Cherokee Indians, as our national melodies. These are no more to us as a people, or even as a nation, because they are

---

* Henry Purcell, it is true, had some semblance of musical inspiration. But even he wrote not a single air which is remembered and sung out of England. The prophets of English music, unlike all others, have their honor in their own country. It may be worth while to add here, that an English critic has remarked that "in all single songs [i.e. airs] till those of Purcell appeared, the principal effects were produced from the *words*, not the *melody*; for the English airs antecedent to Purcell's time [he composed 1682-1695] were as misshapen as if they had been composed of notes scattered about by chance, instead of being cast in a regular mould." The same writer adds, "had his short life been protracted, we might, perhaps, have had a school of secular music of our own which we cannot to this day boast of." And since that day, with the exception of a clever composition or two by Dr. Arne and Sir Henry Bishop, we have been wise enough to let the Italians, Germans, and French write music for us.

* † "When a foreigner asks and inquires about national melodies, he is unanimously (?) directed to hear the so-called negro melodies."— Gurowski's *America and Europe*, p. 179.

heard in this country, than the songs of the birds or the howling of the wolves. We have no national melodies; nor has there been either occasion or mode by which we should obtain them. It seems also pretty sure that we shall never have them. For national melodies are the nursery songs of a people, heard in the dimly recollected days of its infancy, lingering in its maturer memory, and cherished there even more for the sake of dear associations than for their inherent power of pleasing. But this nation was born of full age.

So people demand of us a national literature. But there shall no national literature be given them. What semblance of reason have they for asking it? We have not existed long enough as a nation to produce a distinctive literature. And, in any case, what have political forms, where the essence of liberty is preserved, to do with literature? Something, but very little; and that regarding the mere husk of it. As a people, we have a grand literature, stretching as it does for five hundred years and more, through Milton and Shakspeare, back to Chaucer and Wicliffe; and occupied, as we must needs be, chiefly with the material interests of life, our share of contributions to that literature, in the last fifty years, is one, of which, neither as to its quality nor its quantity, need we be ashamed. Irving, Dana, Bryant, Prescott, Webster, Everett, Longfellow, Poe, Hawthorne, Whittier, Holmes, Lowell, Motley, not to mention others, write good English words, and think good English thoughts. They are, with a single exception, quite as highly appreciated, and perhaps as much read in the mother country as here; while Scott and Bulwer, Wordsworth and Tennyson, Macaulay and Grote, Lamb, Dickens, and Thackeray, have ten readers here, and Shakspeare twenty, for one across the water. De Quincey and Carlyle met their recognition in America; and, on the other hand, Longfellow attained his present eminence first in England.

Strangely enough, as some people call negro songs American national music, others meet the demand for a national literature, by referring the inquirer to "our" Indian legends—the traditions of a savage people which is vanishing away before our race, with which it has not even a single point of affinity or of contact! I have even seen Mr. Longfellow's "Hiawatha" welcomed by a foreign critic as something "at last truly American." And does subject determine nationality? Alas, then, for the English claim to thirteen of Shakspeare's fourteen comedies, and to eleven of his twelve tragedies! These people who call for a distinctive American literature, should be very careful that their children are not born in stables, lest they should turn out to be horses or—something else.

As to the arts of design, in landscape painting—the special development of that art in this age—we have already attained peculiar excellence. But this is the result of local physical causes which do not operate upon music and literature.

English literature is the literature both of the Anglo-Britons and the Anglo-Americans. Its wealth is common to them as a people; and even as nations neither can set up a separate claim that is a century old. The time may come, two or three hundred years hence, when there will be a distinctive American literature,—though not founded upon Indian legends. But even this is doubtful; for in all that might be relied upon to produce a distinctive character in our thought, or even in our language, England is overtaking us faster than we are getting away from her.*

---

* It is needful to remark here upon what is meant by the words 'nation' and 'people' respectively. Within a comparatively short period, necessity, which rules nowhere more despotically than in language, has perverted the former to a sense almost the converse of that which etymologically belongs to it, which implies a mere community of birth and blood, and by natural consequence, identity of language and customs. To these notions of the elements of nationality there came to be added, quite as naturally, those of existence in the same country and under the same government. Thus Sir William Temple says: "A nation properly signifies a great number of families derived from the same blood, born in the same country, and living under the same government." Crabbe, however, the author of "English Synonymes," excludes entirely the elements of country and government from nationality. He says (in not very clear language): "The Americans, when spoken of in relation to Britain, are a distinct people, because they have each a distinct government; but they are not a distinct nation, because they have a common descent." And William Taylor, of Norwich, a far better scholar and closer thinker than Crabbe, in his English Synonymes, thus discriminates between nation and people. "Nation makes the connexion of *birth*, and people that of *common subordination*. * * * A nation is a great family; a people a great corporation. We do not yet [A. D. 1856] oppose the American nation to the British nation, because the ties of kindred, the marks of common birth and descent, are not yet withdrawn; but we oppose the American people to the British people, because the ties of common subordination are wholly cut asunder. The word *nation* excludes, the word *people* includes foreign residents." This is very true etymologically; but it does not meet the linguistic needs either of statesmen or the general public. Etymologically speaking, there is no British nation (except in Wales), but a British people made up of the English, Scotch, Welsh, and Irish nations. But by what code does Great Britain regulate her foreign intercourse, international law or interpopular law? Is the British flag the national or the popular standard, and "God Save the King" the national or the popular hymn? Of necessity, therefore, we find the London *Times*, for instance, speaking continually of the British nation. And Vattel, using 'nation' as synonymous with 'state,' says: "Nations, or States, are political bodies, societies of men united together to attain mutual safety and advantage by their combined strength." Walker ("American Law," pp. 717, 718) says: "By a nation, in the sense in which I am now using the term, I understand a society of people so organized as to govern themselves independently of foreign powers. * * * Thus the American colonies before the Revolution, were only parts of the British nation. And in like manner, the States of the Union are not nations, because they have parted with many of the attributes of independent self-government, but only parts of that one and entire nation, known and recognised by other nations as the United States," &c. Webster's definition of nation is, "A body of people inhabiting the same country, or united under the same sovereign or government;" and in this sense the word is now used by the best writers and speakers in all languages, as well as by people generally. But what then becomes of the nationality which distinguishes the English, the Scotch, and the Irish from each other? What becomes of the nationality of manners, customs, and music? I think that it will be found that the definitions given by Crabbe and Mr. Taylor, must be, nay, to all intents and purposes are, directly reversed; and that we speak of the English people, the Welsh people, the Scotch people, and the Irish people, as forming the British nation; and that Scotch and Irish national airs, for instance, have become Scotch and Irish popular airs, as having originated and been preserved among the Scotch and Irish people. So, although the Jewish nation and Jewish nationality are utterly destroyed, the Jews are, and ever will be, as they, from the days of Moses and Aaron, ever have been, "a peculiar people."

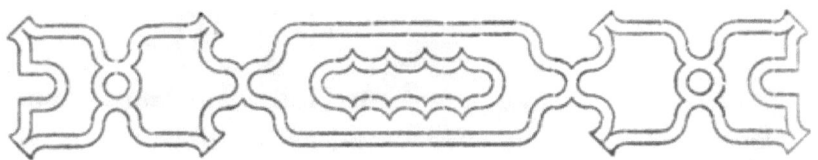

III.

We have, then, no national music, as we have no national literature. But to a national hymn, a national music is not essential; for the British (it never was the English) national hymn is the finest in existence, and that was produced in England, which is as barren of melody as America. The germ of the air is not of English growth; but the thing as a whole is of English fabrication. The music, in the present form of its melody and harmony, is in certain points superior, even to Haydn's noble air, written for the Austrian national hymn, which a true-born Briton, comparing the two, has naively said, "wants the manly, majestic, full-hearted boldness of the strains in which we are accustomed to express, not more our respect for our monarch than our own national pride." The words, indeed, are poor enough. Lyrically, they are naught; but they express in strong, blunt language, the British national feeling; they denounce the king's enemies roundly, and rate them in good set terms; and they do this in the form of prayer to God. They have thus become, by mingled fitness and association, the most absolute expression of John Bull-ism, and so are sung with equal gusto by your true Briton before a big battle, and after a big dinner.

But this fine national air, and its well-suited words, were they written for a coronation, or a victory, or in a general way to express " not more our respect for our monarch than our own national pride?" By whom were they written, and when, and on what inspiration? These points were long mooted, but they have been pretty nearly settled; and before we are done with the subject, we trust that there will be no doubt left upon the question: for the history of this hymn is so curious and instructive that it is worth our attention.

"God Save the King," then, which has become the recognised British national hymn, the concentrated expression of loyalty to King, Lords, and Commons, is, words and music, a rebel composition, written in honor of a pretender to the British throne; and the "enemies" that it so denounces are the reigning House of Hanover, and its supporters. It has been attributed to Dr. John Bull, a musician who lived in England in the reigns of Elizabeth and James I.; but this could have been done only by persons entirely unacquainted with Bull's compositions, which are formal, dry, and dreary to the last degree, besides being "impossible" enough to please Dr. Johnson.*

* The story told of him by Wood, in his *Fasti Oxonienses*, and which is repeated even at this day, that he made himself known to a musi-

It was even said, upon the authority of a Dr. Cook, who had inspected the Archives of the Academy of Ancient Music upon this subject, to have been "written by a Dr. Rogers, in the time of Henry VIII., prior to the Reformation."* But the truth is, that it has not yet been known a hundred and twenty-five years, or recognised as a British national hymn for seventy-five years. As late as 1796, a correspondent of the Gentleman's Magazine expresses a "wish" that "the song of God save the king, may long cheer the heart of many a loyal subject." The air is originally French, and is still sung by the vine-dressers in the south of France. This air, Henry Carey, a musician who lived in the reign of William and Mary, Anne, and the first Georges, adopted and re-wrote, writing also, and perhaps partly adopting, the verses which are now sung to it, with the exception of two very important words.

"God Save the King," was first published in the Gentleman's Magazine for October, 1745, where it appears, with the music, among the miscellaneous collection of rhyming odds and ends, at the end of the number, merely as "*A Song, for two voices. As sung at both Playhouses.*" The melody of the first strain, and the last bar, is different from, and much inferior

---

cian at St. Omer's, by taking a piece of music in forty parts, and adding forty other parts to it, is even more absurd than the attributing "God save the King" to him. The fact is, as any person who can read a musical score, knows physically impossible. The musical scale does not admit even the first forty parts.

* See the Gentleman's Magazine, 1796. p. 993.

to, the present reading.* The harmony is Dr. Arne's, he having arranged the song, and brought it into public notice at one of the theatres; and hence its publication by Cave in his magazine. Testimony has been produced to show that Henry Carey avowed the authorship of the song once in private. His son, George Savile Carey, set up the same claim for his father, and actually applied to George III. for a pecuniary "gratification" on that account. John Christopher Smith, Handel's well known amanuensis, also asserted that Carey was the composer. In the Gen-

* The change is said to have been made by Dr. Pepusch.

"*A New Song for two voices. As sung at both Playhouses.*"

Thus the music of this song is given in the Gentleman's Magazine. The musical reader will notice how important the changes are, and how great the improvements which have been made both in its melody and harmony since that time.

tleman's Magazine for 1795, p. 907, a correspondent complains of the "extreme pains lately taken to degrade the excellent old melody 'God save great George our king,' by attributing it to Henry Carey; a very pleasant well humored fellow, and a good composer, but too much of a buffoon to be the parent of an offspring of such awful deportment." Carey's claim to the authorship of this famous song, has been recently scouted in England by distinguished musical writers.* But there are circumstances, and strong internal evidence, which sustain the testimony in favor of Carey; and in a way which accounts for his never having owned the song publicly himself.

In the Gentleman's Magazine, the first line of the song, which is called "a new song" in the Index, is, of course,

"God save great George, our king."

But as the song grew in favor, it began to be said by some people that, when *they* first heard it, it began—

God save great *James*, our king.

And indubitable evidence was produced, that such was its first form. But there had not been any King James in England since one dark night in 1688! So what did all this mean? The only "person of the name of James," whom any one in England could have asked to have kept particularly safe as king, between 1688 and 1745, was either the dethroned James II.

---

* See, for instance, Mr. George Hogarth's remarks in Home's "Book of British Song." London, 1845, p. 3.

who died in 1701, or his son James, the first Pretender. The song, then, is a Jacobite song; and the enemies, against whose politics and knavish tricks it is so devoutly damnatory are, as before said, the grandfathers, in various degrees of greatness, of her present Most Gracious Majesty. This has been before hesitatingly asserted, and stoutly denied in England;* but, it would seem, after a very partial examination of the subject; for at this very day the song, strangely enough, still retains evidence in support of its Jacobite origin, and also of the period at which it was produced. This evidence appears in the first and second stanzas, the former of which was thus sung, during the reign of the Georges—

> God save great George our king!
> Long live our noble king!
>   God save the king!
> Send him victorious,
> Happy and glorious,
> Long to reign over us,
>   God save the king!

The advent of William and of Victoria to the throne, whose names would not fit the verse, made a change in the first line necessary, which is now sung,

> "God save *our gracious Queen!*"

and this form will probably be preserved hereafter, adapted to the sex of the monarch, omitting the

---

* See Chappell's "Collection of National English Airs." Vol. I. p. 83.

proper name. But while they were making alterations, it is strange indeed that one word was passed over. The neglect must have happened either from sheer oversight, or from the unwillingness to change, even from worse to better, which has become such a distinctive trait of brother Bull's character. The word in question is in the fourth line of the stanza: "*Send* her (or him) victorious, * * * long to reign over us." Send her whence and whither? Why, Victoria, William, George is there: in England: on the throne. It is as plain as the nose on a Bourbon's face that the king for whom that prayer was first sent up, was not within the narrow seas. He was over the water. This is made the surer by the form in which the stanza in question was first written, according to the testimony of those who had heard it sung before 1745, which is supported by interesting collateral evidence.

> " *Send* him victorious,
> Happy and glorious,
> *Soon* to reign over us,
> God save the King!"

This king, very clearly, had not arrived, but was expected; and his faithful subjects were impatient. But rather equivocal—and yet rather unequivocal—words these, to be singing in the year of grace, 1740, in the thirteenth year of the reign of our gracious lord and sovereign King George II., son and rightful heir of his most gracious majesty George I., of happy memory. The incongruity is said to have been seen by the **composer himself,** who sang the song in 1740, at a dinner given at a tavern in Cornhill, in honor of Admiral Vernon's capture of Porto Bello. He then changed "soon" to "long," and owned the song as his composition. But neither Carey, nor, strange to say, those who have since manipulated the song,* seem to have seen the full

* The following is the form in which the song is now sung.

1.

God save our gracious Queen!
Long live our noble Queen!
    God save the Queen!
Send her victorious,
Happy and glorious,
Long to reign over us,
    God save the Queen!

2.

O Lord, our God, arise,
Scatter her enemies,
    And make them fall!
Confound their politics,
Frustrate their knavish tricks,
On her our hopes we fix,
    O save us all!

3.

Thy choicest gifts in store
On her be pleased to pour,
    Long may she reign!
May she defend our laws,
And ever give us cause,
To sing with heart and voice,
    God save the Queen!

In the last line but one of the last stanza, "To *sing* with heart and voice," originally stood "To *say* with heart and voice."

significance of the stanza; for while "soon" was stricken out, "send," the twin tell-tale, and the first-born and louder-voiced of the two, was left, and has been prating, open-mouthed, of his bastardy, for a hundred and twenty years. And even now, if the inappropriateness of the neglected word should be noticed in the proper official quarter, so much does John Bull prefer his *mumpsimus*, **that** he is used to, to a *sumpsimus*, that common **sense** shows **to** be right; **so** reluctant **is** he to change **for the** better, **that** it is more than probable that the obvious correction **to be** made—" *Grant* her victorious "—will not be made, and that we shall hear him praying, "with heart and voice," for the very monarch to be *sent* to him, under whose glorious reign he is so happy as to be **living**.

But the second stanza gives evidence even more strongly than the first, though not quite so palpably, **to** the Jacobite origin of this song:—

   "O Lord our God arise,
    Scatter his enemies,
     And make them fall!
   Confound their **politics**,
   Frustrate their knavish tricks,
   On him our hopes **we fix**,
    God save **us all**!"

Merely observing the pitiful tameness of "**And make them fall**," and the ludicrous bluntness of the **two following lines**, remark particularly that this stanza concerns itself about a king who is in personal peril, from enemies open and secret, and who, with his faithful subjects, is awaiting deliverance. God is called upon not to " scatter his enemies " generally, but to arise, then and there, and do it quickly. The singers do not fix their trust upon the king, but their " hopes ; " and deliverance is expected, longed for, and not only for him :—" God save us *all !* " See, too, in this light, the fitness and the significance of those two queer lines—

> " Confound their politics,
> Frustrate their knavish tricks.

Sung under the sceptre of Victoria, or her uncle, or her grandfather, they are relatively as absurd as they are intrinsically ridiculous. But think of them sung at night, in a retired room, over a jorum of punch or a magnum of claret, by a knot of Jacobite fellows, expecting the Pretender, and having in mind the politics of Lord Townshend and the knavish tricks of Walpole ; and although the poetry is made no better, the incongruity disappears.

It is not certain, however, that Carey originated the motive of this song ; and it is not improbable that he derived the form of it, and some of the words, from an old Jacobite song now lost. For the following curious inscription has been discovered upon the drinking-glasses, among the relics preserved in Scotland, of an ancient Jacobite family :—

> " God save the King, I pray !
> God save the King !
> Send him victorious,
> Soon to reign over us !

> God bless the Prince of Wales,
> The true born Prince of Wales,
>   Sent us by Thee!
> Grant us one favor more,
> The King for to restore,
> As thou hast done before,
>   The Familie!" *

Is this the original of Carey's song, or a reminiscence of it? The absence of the name of the king introduced by Carey in the first lines, and the allusion in the latter to the birth of the son of James II., which was regarded by the Jacobites as a special interposition of Providence, and by the Whigs as too nearly miraculous to be believed in, seem to point it out as of the very earliest Jacobite origin, and written probably in the first years of the reign of William and Mary, as the king mentioned is plainly James himself, who lost the battle of the Boyne in 1690, and died in 1701. As Carey died by his own hand three years before the Jacobite insurrection of 1745, he probably composed what Mr. George Hogarth calls "this noble strain of patriotic loyalty," in 1714 or 1715, when the landing of the Pretender was anxiously expected by all parties, and the writ of *habeas corpus* was suspended.

Many additional stanzas have been written to "God Save the King," but none of them have established themselves as a part of the hymn. One of them is sufficiently comical to be worth noticing. It was written during the second British civil war of the

---

* From Clarke's " Dissertation on God Save the King."

last century, and after the first victories of the young Pretender, against whom was sent, among other commanders, General Wade, an officer from whom much was expected. So the lieges added a stanza to their loyal song, and sang it at both the playhouses, beginning :—

> " Lord, grant that Marshal Wade
> May, by thy mighty aid,
> Victory bring."

A petition that brings to mind some of those put-up now-a-days in New England, in which the petitioners, not content to ask for daily bread, or other benefits in general terms, send up with their prayers special intimations of the mode in which they might most conveniently, or at least agreeably, be granted. For manifestly Wade is the individual mainly looked to; and the mighty aid plainly has its chief value in rhyming with the Marshal's name, and in furnishing also a parenthetical conscience-saver, or assurance of distinguished consideration in the other quarter.

Not Marshal Wade, but the Duke of Cumberland brought victory. And, apropos of victories and defeats in the "unholy civil war" of the times when the British national hymn was coming into vogue, fought about a mere matter of government by "fratricidal" hands, and not malapropos of certain defeats about these times, and what has been said of them, it is worth while to read over those brief passages of British history.

Sept. 1745. "With this reinforcement, his troops [Sir John Cope's, commander of the royal forces] amounted to near *three thousand* men; and he began his march to Edinburgh in order to give battle to the enemy. * * * Early next morning he was attacked by the young Pretender at the head of about *two thousand four hundred* highlanders, *half armed*, who charged him sword in hand with such impetuosity that in *less than ten minutes* after the battle began the King's troops were broken and totally routed. The dragoons *fled in the utmost confusion at the first onset:* the *general officers* having made some unsuccessful efforts to rally them thought proper to *consult their own safety by an expeditious retreat* towards Coldstream on the Tweed. All the infantry were either killed or taken; and their colors, artillery, tents, baggage and military chest fell into the hands of the victor, who returned in triumph to Edinburgh. * * * Not above fifty of the rebels lost their lives in the engagement. Five hundred of the King's troops were killed on the field of battle."
—Smollet's "History of England," vol. iii. p. 143. ed. 1827.

Jan. 1746. "By this time a considerable body of forces were assembled at Edinburgh under conduct of General Hawley, who determined to relieve Stirling Castle. * * * Such was his obstinacy, self-conceit, or contempt of the enemy, that he slighted the repeated intelligence he had received of their motions and design, firmly believing they durst not hazard an engagement. * * * The highlanders kept up their fire, and took aim so well that the assailants were *broke by the first volley; they retreated with precipitation.* * * * The rebels followed their first blow, and the great part of the royal army, after one irregular discharge, *turned their backs and fled in the utmost consternation.*"
—*Idem. Ibid.* p. 153.

After the battle of Manassas it would be very presuming in an American to say anything about panics, or to discuss the question whether the regular troops of any other than a pusillanimous people could flee panic-stricken from less than their own number of half-armed volunteers; and so these passages present a difficulty which must be passed over in silence. But the historian helps us a little by telling us that in April following, these very thrice-victorious rebel volunteers, "having been under arms during the whole preceding night," and being "faint with hunger and fatigue, and many of them overpowered with sleep," were routed at the battle of Culloden, in the famous slaughter at which, by the way, Hawley and his troops did distinguished service.

> "In less than thirty minutes they were totally defeated, and the field covered with the slain. The road as far as Inverness, was strewed with dead bodies; and a great number of people who, from motives of curiosity, had come to see the battle, were sacrificed to the undistinguishing vengeance of the victors."—*Ib. Id.*, p. 159.

Events never repeat themselves exactly; but there is sometimes a striking similarity between them; so striking that it is hardly safe, whatever happens, for a people to say, "We never did," or "we never would do so. Look at us; be humiliated, and take example." Americans should remember this, and lay the lesson well to heart.

But to return to the new song which some Englishmen were singing at both the playhouses about the time of these battles for the success of King George, while some others—these, too, the "real original Jacob-ites"—were singing it at their own houses for the success of King James.—A time, Mr. Punch when, O grinning puppet, jerked into antics with strings mostly of a three-penny value, and with a single eye upon the crowd through which the hat is passing,—

> British Jacobites were pot,
> And loyal British, kettle,
> Equal morally, if not
>   Men of equal mettle.*

---

* See the following stanza in Punch upon "The Run from Manassas Junction."

The majestic beauty of the music of "God Save the King" has won it a singular distinction which is quite inconsistent with one of the functions of a national air. It has been adopted for the national hymns of Prussia, Hanover, Weimar, Brunswick, and Saxony; so that its distinctive nationality is no longer in its music, but only in its poor, perverted, rebel-born words.

> "We for North and South alike
>   Entertain affection.
> These for Negro slavery strike,
>   Those for forced protection.
> Yankee Doodle is the pot,
>   Southerner the kettle,
> Equal morally, if not
>   Men of equal mettle.

And so slavery and a high tariff are now equal morally in John Bull's eyes! The admission of what the whole world more than suspected has come at last. Its candor, not to say effrontery, gives it some claim upon admiration. And is it thus that Britain stands confessed before us! Britain indeed; but, alas, how much changed from that Britain that decked herself in the spoils of slavery, and hurled the fires of consuming vengeance upon the inhuman fleets!

IV.

The history of the other great national hymn of the world, the Marseillaise—for these two separate themselves by eminence from all the others—is noticeably and significantly unlike that which has just been examined. Every reader of this little book may not know all the brief history of that marvellous song, which is almost travestied in Lamartine's sentimental melodramatic account of it in the *Girondins*. It received its name from the men who first made it known in Paris, the ruffian Marseillais.—a horde, some five hundred strong, of the vilest and most brutal of the floating population of a Mediterranean sea-port town, who were summoned to Paris by Barbaroux for the purpose of exciting and assisting at the atrocities of 1792. Headed by the wretch Santerre, they marched into Paris, and through its principal streets, on the 30th of July in that year, a band of swarthy, fierce, travel-soiled desperados, wearing red Phrygian caps wreathed with green leaves, dragging cannon, and singing as they marched, a song beginning:

> "Allons, enfans de la patrie,
>   Le jour de gloire est arrivé!
>   Contre nous, de la tyrannie
>   L'etendard sanglant est levé.
>   Entendez vous dans ces campaignes
>   Mugir ces féroces soldats!
>   Ils viennent jusque dans vos bras
>   Egorger vos fils et vos compagnes!—
> Aux armes, citoyens! formez vos bataillons!
> Marchons! qu' un sang impur abreuve nos sillons!"

These inflaming accents were just suited to the intense craving of the morbid appetite created by the revolution; they at once stimulated and gratified, though they could not slake it; and on that day Paris drank in with greedy ears an intoxication from which, in spite of certain seeming intervals of imposed restraint, she has been reeling ever since.

But who had done this? Not a Marseillais, not a *sans-culotte*, not even a revolutionist. Rouget de Lisle was none of these, but an accomplished officer, an enthusiast for liberty it is true, but no less a champion of justice, and an upholder of constitutional monarchy. He was at Strasbourg early in 1792. One day Dietrich, the mayor of the town, who knew him well, asked him to write a martial song to be sung on the departure of six hundred volunteers who would soon set out to join the army of the Rhine. De Lisle consented, wrote the song that night—the words sometimes coming to him before the music, sometimes the music before the words—and gave it to Dietrich the next morning. As is not uncommon with authors, he was at first dissatisfied with the fruit of his sudden inspiration, and as he handed the manuscript to the mayor, he said, "Here is what you asked for; but I fear it is not very good." But Dietrich looked, and knew better. They went to the harpsichord with Madame and sang it; they gathered the band of the theatre together and rehearsed it; it was sung in the public square, and excited such enthusiasm that, instead of six hundred volunteers, nine hundred left Strasbourg for the army. This song its author called merely "The War-Song of the Army of the Rhine" (*Chant de guerre de l'armée du Rhin*). But in the course of a few months it worked its way southwards, and became a favorite with the Marseillais, who carried it to Paris, where the people, knowing nothing of its name, its author, or its original purpose, spoke of it simply as "the Song of the Marseillais," and as the Marseillaise it will be known for ever, and for ever be the rallying cry of France against tyranny.

How widely do the histories of these two hymns differ, and how characteristic is their difference of the two people who have adopted them! The British hymn, like the British constitution, the product of no man and of no time; the origin of its several parts various and uncertain, or seen darkly through the obscurity of the past; its elements the product of different peoples; broached at first in secret, and when brought to light, frowned down as treasonable, heretical, damnable; but at length openly avowed, and gradually growing into favor; modified, curtailed, added to in important points by various hands, yet remaining vitally untouched; at last accepted because it is no longer prudent to refuse to yield it place; and finally insisted upon as the time-honored palladium of British liberty. The Marseillaise, written to order, and in one night, to meet a sudden, imperative demand: struck out at the white heat of unconscious inspiration, perfect in all its parts, *totus, teres, atque rotundus;* and in six months adopted by the people, the army, and the legislature of the whole nation. The air of the one, simple, solid, vigorous, dignified, grand, the music of common sense and fixed determination; the words, though poor enough, mingling trust, and prayer, and self-confidence, and respect for whoever is above us, and a readiness to fight stoutly when God and the law are on our side: the other a war cry, a summons to instant battle, warning, appealing, denouncing, fiercely threatening the vengeance of the Furies; having no inspiration but glory, and invoking no god but liberty; beginning in deliberate enthusiasm, and ending in conscious frenzy.

How different the service too, to which the two songs have been put! The one used always to sustain, to build up, to perpetuate, to express loyalty and faithful endurance; a song of peace and plethoric festivity. The other, the signal of destruction, the warning note of revolution; the song that rises from the field where the red ploughshare turns up petrified abuses to the light of heaven and vengeance stalks between the stilts; the howl of famished men, and the shriek of nursing mothers whose breasts are dry. The one at best a tonic, but mostly sedative in its operation, and harmless at any time: the other from the beginning a stimulant, and to be used on great occasions only, and for great objects. The Girondists sang the first four lines of it, as—except one who fell before his judges, struck through the heart with his own dagger—they turned away from the bloody tribunal which had condemned them to death in the name of the liberty they had done so much to gain. At the battle of Jemappes, at the most perilous hour of that long doubtful day, Dumouriez, finding his right wing almost without officers, and giving way before the fire of the Austrian infantry and a threatened charge of the huzzars, put himself at the head of his battalions and began to sing the Marseillaise hymn, then not many months old; the soldiers joined in the song, their courage rallied, they charged and carried all before them. And in August of the next year at the fête of the inauguration of the constitution (always a fête and an inauguration!) when the convention and the delegates from the primary assemblies, including eighty-six *doyens*—which seems to be French for the oldest inhabitant—to represent the eighty-six departments, assembled with a throng of "citizens generally" in the *Place de la Bastille* at four o'clock in the morning around a great fountain, called the Fountain of the Regeneration, as soon as the first beams of the sun appeared, they saluted him by singing stanzas to the air of the Marseillaise; and then the President took a cup, poured out before the sun the waters of regeneration, and drank thereof himself, and passed the cup to the oldest inhabitants, and they also drank thereof, in their parochial capacity. These ways are not the ways of our race. Indeed, even if Sir John Cope had begun to sing "God Save the King" at Preston-pans, or General Hawley had in like manner lifted up his voice at Falkirk, or General McDowell had favored the army with the "Star-Spangled Banner" at Manassas (always supposing it to be within the compass of his voice), I doubt much whether they would have produced any change in the fortunes of those battles; nay I fear they would have been greeted only with unseemly merriment. Sir John Cope's regulars would still have "fled in the utmost confusion at the first onset;" General Hawley's veterans would have been "broke by the first volley" and "turned their backs and fled in the utmost consternation;" and General McDowell's raw volunteers, after fighting three hours and a half against an entrenched enemy in superior force, and driving him a two miles before them, would still have been seized with a sudden panic and retreated in disgraceful disorder to Washington, leaving their enemy so crippled that he could not, even if he dared, pursue them.*

But differing thus entirely in spirit and origin, these celebrated songs have one historical point in common,

* See the extracts from Southern newspapers and letters in the "Rebellion Record."

which is interesting in itself, and full of significance to such folk as say, Go to, let us make a national hymn:—they have both been perverted from their original purpose. The British hymn, made up, as we have seen, of an air from France, and words from Jacobite Scotland, into a song praying for the scattering, the confounding, the frustrating, and the general damnation of the reigning family, with its words altered by this man and the other, and its melody doctored by this musician and its harmony by the other, has come to be the recognised formal expression of loyalty to the very house for whose overthrow it first petitioned. And as to the Marseillaise, the purpose of its author is sadly told in his sad fate. Soon proscribed as a royalist, he fled from France, and took refuge in the Alps. But the echoes of the chord that he so unwittingly had struck pursued him even to the mountain tops of Switzerland. "What," said he to a peasant guide in the upper fastnesses of the border range, "is this song that I hear—*Allons, enfans de la patrie?*" "That? That is the Marseillaise." And thus, suffering from the excesses that he had innocently stimulated, he first learned the name which his countrymen had given to the song that he had written.*

* I have reason to believe that complete copies of the Marseillaise Hymn are not so common as to make a reproduction of the whole song unwelcome here. Most copies contain only three stanzas, the first, second, and sixth, and those only are sung as the national hymn; but the third, fourth, and fifth, are interesting from the marks they bear of the occasion on which they were written. In the fifth, there is even a denunciation of Marshal Bouillé, by name:—

But from the purpose built into its very structure, and breathing in its every word, the Marseillaise can-

CHANT DE GUERRE DE L'ARMÉE DU RHIN.

BY ROUGET D'LISLE.

1.

Allons, enfans de la patrie,
Le jour de gloire est arrivé!
Contre nous, de la tyrannie
L'étendard sanglant est levé.
Entendez-vous dans ces campagnes
Mugir ces féroces soldats!
Ils viennent jusque dans vos bras
Egorger vos fils et vos compagnes!—
Aux armes, citoyens! formez vos bataillons!
Marchons! qu'un sang impur abreuve nos sillons!

2.

Que veut cette horde d'esclaves,
De traitres, de rois conjurés?
Pour qui ces ignobles entraves,
Ces fers dès longtemps preparés?
Français, pour vous; ah, quel outrage!
Quels transports il doit exciter!
C'est vous qu'on ose méditer
De rendre à l'antique esclavage.
Aux armes, citoyens! formez vos bataillons!
Marchons! qu'un sang impur abreuve nos sillons!

3.

Quoi! ces cohortes étrangères
Feraient la loi dans nos foyers?
Quoi? ces phalanges mercenaires
Terrasseraient nos pères guerriers.
Grand Dieu! par des mains enchainées,
Nos fronts sous le joug se ploieraient;
Des vils despots deviendraient
Les maitres de nos destinées!
Aux armes, citoyens! formez vos bataillons!
Marchons! qu'un sang impur abreuve nos sillons!

not be perverted. It is a war song, and is only suited to the periods when the liberties of the nation are threatened. Therefore, other national airs are per-

4.

Tremblez, tyrans! et vous, perfides,
L'opprobre de tous les partis!
Tremblez, vos projets parricides
Vont enfin recevoir leur prix!
Tout est soldat pour vous combattre:
S'ils tombent nos jeunes héros,
La France en produit des nouveaux,
Contre vous tout prêts à se battre.
Aux armes, citoyens! formez vos bataillons!
Marchons! qu'un sang impur abreuve nos sillons!

5.

Français, en guerriers magnanimes,
Portez ou retenez vos coups;
Épargnez ces tristes victimes,
A regret s'armant contre vous.
Mais ces despotes sanguinaires,
Mais ces complices de Bouillé,
Tous ces tigres sans pitié,
Dechirent le sein de leur mère.
Aux armes, citoyens! formez vos bataillons.
Marchons! qu'un sang impur abreuve nos sillons!

6.

Amour sacré de la patrie,
Conduis, soutiens nos bras vengeurs!
Liberté, liberté chérie,
Combats avec tes defenseurs!
Sous nos drapeaux que la Victoire
Accoure à tes mâles accents;
Que tes ennemis expirants
Voient ton triomphe et notre gloire!
Aux armes, citoyens! formez vos bataillons!
Marchons! qu'un sang impur abreuve nos sillons!

STRASBOURG, 1792.

formed on ordinary occasions. "*Partant pour la Syrie*," attributed to Queen Hortense, is, with no special propriety, the recognised French air at present. "God save the King" has the advantage of being suited to all times and seasons; so while there is a king in Great Britain no other song will take its place. And this will be a very long time; much longer than many people think. For not only is John Bull, as I heard a distinguished British statesman say, "a lord-loving animal; he is a king-worshipping creature also. He may daily devote his own soul to perdition, but he devoutly prays for the queen and all the royal family. He delights in the very epithet royal, and unless some of his heartiness is bred out of him, utters it with unctuous relish. He rises in his own respect by dealing with the grocer to her Majesty; and his eye beams complacently upon the crown stamped on his pickle jar. Kingship will never be driven out from that land; it will be solicitously retained while it is gradually robbed of even the semblance of prerogative, until at length there will be somebody called a king there who has less power than a constable. And when at last the shadow of royalty has become so faint that even British eyes can see nothing on the throne but velvet and vacuity, and nothing in the crown but emptiness, when the game of monarchy is played out, and "God Save the King" cannot be sung because there is no king to save, be sure that a new national hymn will not be written. The old air will be preserved; the words will be altered as little as possible, and perverted as much as possible, so that

Britons, though they no longer express their "respect for their monarch," can yet give utterance to their "national pride," as nearly as may be in the good old way.*

* A gentleman who has seen the proofs of these pages as they passed through the press, has laid upon my table the following verses as a rough sketch of the form which the British national hymn might conveniently take at the period referred to above:—

GOD SAVE JOHN BULL.

God save me, great John Bull!
Long keep my pocket full!
    God save John Bull!
Ever victorious,
Haughty, vain-glorious,
Snobbish, censorious,
    God save John Bull!

O Lords, our gods, arise!
"Tax" all our enemies,
    Make tariffs fall!
Confound French politics,
Frustrate all Russian tricks,
Get Yankees in a "fix,"
    God "bless" them all!   [*Sinistrâ manu.*]

Thy choicest gifts in store,
On me, me only pour,—
    Me, great John Bull!
Maintain oppressive laws,
Frown down the poor man's cause!
So sing with heart and voice,
    I, great John Bull.

But rough as this sketch is, I cannot present it even thus, without expostulating with my friend on his grave, and I fear mischievous misrepresentations of the British character and policy. I must protest against it, also, as an ungrateful return for the candor, the courtesy, and the genuine good feeling with which American affairs have always, and especially of late, been discussed in Great Britain.

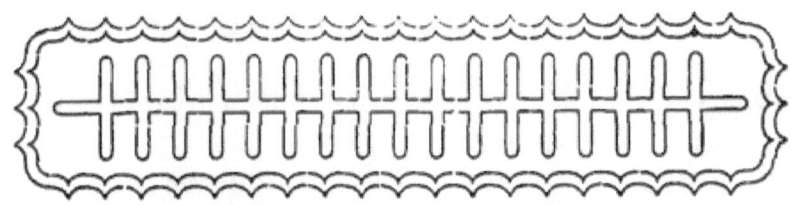

V.

Less fortunate as we are than British subjects and French citizens, in having no national hymn, the history of theirs is not very encouraging to an attempt to obtain one deliberately. But in that need of one which was felt just after the breaking out of our great pro-slavery insurrection, a number of gentlemen were requested to act as a committee to offer a prize for the words and music of a hymn which, in their judgment, might be to us something like what the British and French hymns are to those nations. It has been said that this committee was self-appointed; but that was not the case. The notion of thus calling for a national hymn, I know did not even originate with any member of the committee, but with an intelligent gentleman whose warm patriotic feeling led him to be active in the matter. At first it was proposed to place the matter in the hands of three gentlemen, one from New York, Boston, and Philadelphia, respectively; but the inconvenience of this plan soon became apparent, and the New York committee was appointed. All who were asked heartily consented to serve; but not one of them expressed any confidence in the success of the undertaking. Yet as there was a great desire expressed for the hymn on all sides, and as the occasion was propitious for its production, they willingly said Yes, instead of No. They felt much like the Bowery boy who, being cut short in a hard life by a sore disease, which quickly brought him to death's door, was informed by his physician that medicine could do nothing for him. "What's my chances, doctor?" "Not worth speaking of." "One in twenty?" "Oh, no." "In thirty?" "No." "Fifty?" "I think not." "A hundred?" "Well, perhaps there may be one in a hundred." "I say, then, doctor," pulling him close down, and whispering with feeble earnestness in his ear, "jess you go in like h— on that one chance." The doctor "went in," and the patient recovered. The chance that there was, the members of the committee did not feel at liberty to refuse.

There was special reason, too, at the time of the appointment of the committee, for the hope that it might accomplish its object. The excited feeling of the country vented itself in verse to a most remarkable extent. Newspapers which undertook to gather these effusions of popular sentiment together from various quarters, filled column after column with them, and sometimes page after page. The greater part of these verses were unmitigated nonsense, it is true; much of the residue was commonplace; but really spirited and well-written compositions appeared with sufficient frequency, considering what a very rare production good lyric poetry is, to give color to the hope that from some poet of reputation, or from some other who had his reputation to make, the wished-for song would come.

The following verses were written about that time. The reader will remember how intently the whole country had watched Fort Sumter through four long months (it seems as if it had been four years, and had happened twenty years ago!) and with what intense feeling they learned that Major Anderson had struck his flag when the fort became untenable, and had evacuated, not surrendered, the post, raising his flag again and saluting it; and this happening on Saturday, how on Monday morning the eye could hardly turn, north of the Potomac, without being gladdened by the sight of the American flag,—how dear to us, we of this generation never knew till then!

THE FLAG.

BY HORATIO WOODMAN.

Why flashed that flag on Monday morn
   Across the startled sky?
Why leapt the blood to every cheek,
   The tears to every eye?
The hero in our four months' woe,
   The symbol of our might,
Together sunk for one brief hour,
   To rise for ever bright.

The mind of Cromwell claimed his own,
   The blood of Naseby streamed

Through hearts unconscious of the fire,
   Till that torn banner gleamed.
The seeds of Milton's lofty thoughts.
   All hopeless of the spring,
Broke forth in joy, as through them glowed
   The life great poets sing.

Old Greece was young, and Homer true,
   And Dante's burning page
Flamed in the red along our flag,
   And kindled holy rage.
God's Gospel cheered the sacred cause,
   In stern, prophetic strain,
Which makes His Right our covenant,
   His Psalms our deep refrain.

Oh, sad for him whose light went out
   Before this glory came,
Who could not live to feel his kin
   To every noble name;
And sadder still to miss the joy
   That twenty millions know,
In Human Nature's Holiday,
   From all that makes life low.

BOSTON, April, 1861.

A condition of the general mind which brought forth on the spur of the occasion a lyric so vigorous, so inspiring, so vividly expressive of the sentiment that stirred the heart of the nation, was surely one from which another, breathing the same spirit in like stirring accents, and of general application, might reasonably be hoped. And so the committee cast out its net, and waited patiently for the dawning. Not only, however, was all not to be fish that came to that net, but, like the cat-fishing negro who rejected with austere self-denial the bass which he found upon his hook, because "when he fished for bass, he fished for bass, but when he fished for catty, he fished for catty," the committee would have what it sought or nothing, no matter how much better fish insisted upon swallowing the bait; and as to getting its "catty," it had the gravest doubts. The prize was therefore not offered for the best hymn that should be written, but for the hymn needed, and if that, in the judgment of the committee, did not come, no matter how much superior "an article" of another style were offered, all were to be rejected.* It is worth while to state

* The following are the call and the conditions of competition published by the committee:

A NATIONAL HYMN.

In obedience to the request of many citizens, who have observed the tendency to give poetic expression to the emotion which stirs the heart of the nation, the gentlemen whose names are undersigned have consented to act as a Committee to award a prize of Five Hundred Dollars for a National Hymn, set to music (either original or selected), upon the following conditions:

1. The Hymn is to be purely patriotic, adapted to the whole country—not a war-song, or only appropriate to the present moment.

2. It must consist of not less than sixteen lines, and is not to exceed forty, exclusive of a chorus or burden, which is essential.

3. It should be of the simplest form and most marked rhythm; the words easy to be retained by the popular memory, and the melody and harmony such as may be readily sung by ordinary voices.

4. For the words and music (whether the latter be original, or selected and adapted) from the same hand, which the Committee would prefer, Five Hundred Dollars, or a gold medal of that value, will be awarded. For the Hymn alone, or for the music alone (if original), Two Hundred and Fifty Dollars, or a gold medal of that value.

5. The Committee retain the copyright of both words and music of the Hymn to which the prize is awarded; and reserve the right of rejecting all contributions, whatever their merit, should none of them be deemed suitable.

6. The profits of the sale of the Hymn are to be devoted to the Patriotic Fund.

this very explicitly; because although it was clearly enough set forth in the committee's proposals, many persons, some of them intelligent enough to know better, if they had read those proposals, have complained of the final decision, as if the committee had done the competitors wrong in not awarding the prize to some one of them. Not a few also, and invariably the authors of those hymns which had the least claim to consideration, seemed to think that the committee was bound to coddle their feelings, to flatter their vanity, and to enter into personal correspondence with them; and in fact that the committee had placed itself under some obligations to competitors: when the real state of the case was that the obligation was all on the other side. The committee merely accepted the responsibility and the labor of examining and

7. The words and music must be furnished by the 20th day of June next.

8. As the Committee may desire to publish a selection from the manuscripts in a volume in aid of the Patriotic Fund, they request those writers who are willing that their productions should be used for that purpose to signify their assent.

9. Individual applications to members of the Committee will be disregarded.

10. Each Hymn offered must be distinguished only by a motto or cipher, and be accompanied by a sealed envelope bearing the same motto or cipher, and containing the writer's name and address. All communications should be addressed to Maunsell B. Field, Esq., Secretary of the National Hymn Committee, New York city.

11. The Committee will return no manuscripts.

GULIAN C. VERPLANCK.	JOHN A. DIX.
CHARLES KING.	M. H. GRINNELL.
HAMILTON FISH.	LUTHER BRADISH.
GEORGE WM. CURTIS.	RICH'D GRANT WHITE.
J. J. CISCO.	JOHN R. BRODHEAD.
GEORGE T. STRONG.	ARTHUR LEARY.

MAUNSELL B. FIELD.

NEW YORK, May 17, 1861.

comparing all the songs that might be sent in, and of deciding whether such a hymn had been sent as in their opinion would meet the public necessity; nothing more.

The call, having been made the subject of newspaper comment throughout the country, met with a response, for the extent of which the committee were not prepared. Nearly twelve hundred competitors appeared upon the field. Manuscripts came from all quarters of the country, including California, nay, even from England, and at last from Italy. The committee went at its work at the earliest moment, and performed it as rapidly as the other engagements of its various members permitted.

The twelve hundred competitors at least, will like to know that this was the manner of proceeding. The manuscripts containing words alone were first opened, the music being laid aside for separate consideration. The verses were then read by the member who opened the envelope containing them. If they were condemned at once by a nearly unanimous voice, they were cast into a waste-basket ready at hand; if not, they were reserved for future consideration. But, by a waste-basket, must not be understood any of those ordinary wicker concavities, known to mortals by that name. A vast washing-basket—a " buck-basket," big enough to hold Falstaff himself—was made the temporary tomb of these extinguished hopes : and this receptacle was filled five times with rejected manuscripts, which were seized upon for incendiary purposes by the cooks of the gentlemen at whose houses the meetings of the Committee took place. Alas, for the hapless writers! Were even the priceless manuscript plays of the Shakespearian age that Warton's cook purloined, and used to put under pies, so lamented as those remorselessly incremated hymns will be? The mass of these manuscripts were "only of interest to their writers," or, in plain terms, either the flattest common-place, or absolutely neither rhyme nor reason. From the whole collection, only about thirty were reserved as worthy of a second reading, and these, on a second and third examination, were reduced about one-half.

The hymns sent in with music were about three hundred in number. To enable them fairly to judge the merits of these, the Committee called in competent musical aid, and after a winnowing of the heap over the piano-forte, those which were found worthy of a more particular hearing were sung. This second examination left less than twenty musical compositions in the hands of the Committee. Among the rejected musical manuscripts were very many that were evidently written by persons who were ignorant of the very first principles of harmony, and who to their ignorance added utter lack of native musical capacity.*

---

* The committee were under obligations, which I venture here to express for them, to Mr. William Scharfenberg, and to Mr. Cutler, Organist of Trinity Church, and some members of the choir of that venerable establishment. These gentlemen placed their time and talents at the service of the committee, with heartiness and alacrity; and though gracefully leaving judgment upon the merits of the compositions placed before them entirely in the hands of the committee, did much to lighten and to aid their labors.

The meetings, except the first and second, were graced and enlivened by the presence of a very few ladies, whose discreet reserve of their opinions did not deprive the committee entirely of the benefit of their quick intelligence and highly cultivated taste. The sportive peremptoriness with which they cried "basket," upon the reading of a song which at once depressed the spirits of the critical tribunal, quite rivalled the pretty austerity with which the Roman ladies turned down their thumbs upon the poor gladiator, who was so weak as to implore their pity instead of conquering their admiration. And slanderous asserters of the curiosity of the sex will blush to learn that these ladies did not even put the committee to the pain of refusing them a single peep into the sealed envelopes containing the authors' names; although the feminine hands upon so many of the queer productions, gave tempting occasion for the indulgence of a little innocent malice, at the expense of a cerulean sister.

But what was the standard by which the hymns were tried? The conditions stated in the first three paragraphs of the committee's proposal were of course insisted on. I venture to say that they are both intrinsically and relatively good; and that no song which does not conform to them will ever be adopted as our national hymn. That it should be purely patriotic and adapted to the whole country in its normal state, no one will dispute. That a mere war song is not needed even by a people who are so eager for military glory as the French, is shown by the fact that they keep their Marseillaise for extraordinary occasions. It has been well said by one of the members of the Committee—Mr. Curtis—" Any truly patriotic national hymn is, of necessity, the great peace song and the great war song of the nation. It fits every emotion of the national heart. It is the national heart-beat set to music." A song of less than sixteen lines cannot well say enough, and one of more than about forty is too long to be remembered. Here the Marseillaise—cut down from the original six to three stanzas—again furnishes illustration and support. A chorus is necessary ; for the main object is that a throng of people may join in the hymn, and it is not reasonable to expect that a miscellaneous crowd of Americans should master the whole of a song, words and music. Nor is it desirable; the effect of contrast in solo and chorus is too fine to lose. That a song, intended to please all, to dwell in all ears, and to suit all ordinary voices, should be simple in melody and harmony, and marked in rhythm, I apprehend that no one will dispute. In these respects, " God Save the King" is a model, unsurpassable, almost unapproachable for us at least. The broken rhythm of the melody of the Marseillaise and the modulations upon which its melody depends, would unfit it for popular singing by a nation of our race. Yet we might well accept a somewhat more spirited, though not less regular, melody than that of " God Save the King."

But these are only the formal, and so to speak the

external conditions of our national hymn. What should be its spirit and its style? Must it needs have **great lyric** excellence? Should it be enriched by imagination and fancy? What should be its motive? For what should it express love and admiration? to what, devotion? What should be the style of its music? These are hard questions. For to prescribe what will suit the public taste and touch the popular heart, is the most delicate, difficult, and uncertain office that could be assumed. No degree of culture, no keenness of perception, not even a high degree of responsive sympathy can insure a happy choice. The chord that will thrill the heart of a nation when struck, however casually, cannot be certainly designated. The most gifted poet or rapt musician might fail to arrest the popular attention when he essayed to sing, not only to the people, but for them; while some chance-uttered strain, expressing only the emotion of a simple, untaught nature, might be caught up, spontaneously adopted, and become the rallying note of a whole nation.

To try a national hymn by a high critical standard; to demand for it an unusual degree of lyric merit, and to insist that **the poetry should be** equal to the **theme,** would be a grave critical error. Such a standard as this is false for any **song that is** written to be sung. "Music married to immortal verse," is a very fine thing for a poet to write about; but an almost impossible thing to find. Apollo seems to have forbidden the bans of that much desired union. There, indeed, are some rare exceptions to this general rule. Of the lovely canzonet, "She never told her love," for instance, the words are by Shakespeare and the music by Haydn. Illustrious conjunction! And yet, although its sentiment is one which all the world must feel, how rarely is it heard! It is remarkable that most popular songs are of very moderate, if not decidedly inferior, poetic merit; and that their music rarely delights ears which listen to songs purely for music's sake; which people of our race generally do not. But they will almost invariably be found to express or suggest some strong sentiment common to the people among whom they are sung, or to bring up vividly some cherished association. Few poorer songs have lived for half a century than "Home, sweet home;" and yet it shall bring tears into a thousand manly eyes on the banks of the Potomac sooner than the most pathetic strain of Pergolesi or Bellini. That the popular taste is sympathetic rather than artistic, must be seen and known of all men. In a song that they can sing with their whole hearts, people to whom music and poetry are not special gifts or acquirements, will forgive faults of structure and language which would drive a critic to despair. And who thinks of or cares for the words of an opera! Unhappy they who should! But there it is the situation or the sentiment alone to which the music must be moulded. *Cuore* and *amore*, "verdant plains" and "happy swains" answer the purpose as well as if Anacreon or Pindar wrote. For music is its own inspiration; and words are but the occasion of its production, and the vehicle of its utterance. Songs which are intrinsically beautiful, like Shakespeare's, for instance, and Herrick's, need no music to complete their lyric expression. They are both words and music, and sing themselves.*

If a high lyric standard is generally false for songs written for music, it is especially so when applied to a national hymn. Lyric beauties are not essential to those songs: nay, the tribunal which passes upon this question seems to have decided that they are hardly admissible. How many noble lyrics have been written by British authors; songs graced with all the beauty of poetic art, aglow with patriotic fervor, and sounding with a pyrrhic clash! But none of them have really attained popularity save Thomson's "Rule Britannia," which has the least poetic merit of them all, which is set to music almost ridiculous, and which has attained its place only by virtue of the arrogant self-assertion of the words, and particularly the precipitate assurance of the chorus that—

"Britons never, never, never, shall be slaves."

And in the Marseillaise there are none of the graces of poetry. With a single exception, not a line con-

* The only song of Shakespeare's which has not been marred by the music to which it is set is that exquisite one in "As You Like It," "Blow, blow, thou winter wind," which Dr. Arne gave fitting voice to by a special and, I believe, an isolated inspiration. As to the music which Locke wrote for the songs in "Macbeth," truly it is manufactured after a very workmanlike fashion; but is otherwise only valuable as an example of the degree of incongruity which there may be between music and the words which the composer believes inspired it. The words are so weird, and the music is so formal and respectable, and with a tie-wig formality and respectability, that the effect of the combination is pure burlesque.

tains a metaphor or a conceit, and that exception is the one blot upon the song; fallen, too, where it shows most, in the last line of the chorus. After the call "*Aux armes, citoyens! Formez vos bataillons!*" and,— with that proud step into the major key—"*Marchons!*" the sequel, "*qu' un sang impur abreuve nos sillons,*" belittles and enfeebles the summons. Men who are in a patriotic frenzy don't stop about impure blood watering their furrows. They go to their object straighter than that. But Rouget d'Lisle needed a rhyme for *bataillons;* we remember that he wrote his war song in one night; and, more than all, the weight of his superfluous trope is borne swiftly from our ken by the mighty sweep of his fire-winged melody.

In a national hymn it is neither the words alone, nor the music alone; it is a felicitous combination of music and poetic interest. This may be attained fortuitously, or at least unconsciously; but attained, it insures immortality, a dwelling-place in the heart of a whole nation. The words must express with fervid directness the central conviction and predominating sentiment of the people. This should have a strong and simple utterance in a verse of four accents; the language being succinct and nervous, the style glowing and lively. Imagination, vivid and robust, may have brief scope; but fancy should have little play, and high finish should not be sought for. To such words there should be written what puritan John Sternhold would call "apt notes to sing them withal." A square melody is the best for the same reason that a verse of four accents is to be preferred, because the ear catches and the memory retains such melody and such verse more easily than any other.*

As to a hymn for Americans, it must of all things proclaim, assert, and exult in the freedom of those who are to sing it. Let this be the expression; let it be brimful of loyalty to the flag, which is our only national symbol, and for that all the dearer; let its allusions be to our fathers' struggle for national existence, and its spirit be that of our nationality; let it have a strong, steady, rhythmical flow; and these points secured as to the words, the air is the most important matter. If that be such a one as all who sing can sing, and as the majority will like, association and habit will accomplish the rest. The music must not be brilliant like an Italian cavatina; or curiously harmonized like a German choral; but simple and strong, with a graceful, lively strength. A song which fulfilled these conditions, and which superadded to their requirements the inspiration that would set them all at naught, or make them entirely superfluous, would pervade and penetrate, and cheer the land like sunlight.

But how hard it is to lay down rules which shall be unfailing guides upon a subject like this, may be.

---

* A square melody is one consisting of four phrases of equal length, the last ending on the harmony on which the first began, or of two or more groups based upon this formula, which will be found to be the model of almost all melodies, either ballad, martial, or operatic, that have become popular. "Auld Lang Syne" is a marked example. The first phrase ends upon the dominant; the second upon the subdominant; the third upon the dominant; and the fourth, of course, upon the tonic, whence the first started.

seen by the following stanza of a hymn which has the air of having been written by one of those gentlemen whom the English journalists and draughtsmen, including those in the employ of "Punch," seem to regard as our representative men.

> We air the greatest nation
> In all the Lord's creation.
>   We air the hull world's wonder,
>   En we hev the loudest thunder
> Accordin' to popilation.

This undeniably conforms to the condition of expressing with directness and strength the convictions and predominating sentiment of at least a certain part of our people, besides stating, in addition, a noticeable fact in our country's physics. It is also manifestly emulous of this stanza of "Rule Britannia."

> "The nations not so blest as thee
>   Must in their turns to tyrants fall;
>   While thou shalt flourish great and free,
> The dread and envy of them all."

But the complacency of the unlettered Yankee has failed to equal the arrogance of the eminent British poet; and as we can admit no inferior merit, a hymn of which this is a specimen, should for that reason alone be rejected. It should be remarked here, that the outcry in England against the closing sentence of Mr. Seward's dispatch of May 4th to Mr. Dayton, in which he said that our nation and government would "stand hereafter as they are now, objects of human wonder and human affection," is manifestly owing to the fact that he stole Thomson's thunder. But he greatly moderated its bellowings. Even in the excitement of the time in which he wrote, and under the provocation which had been received from Europe, he only ventured the not absolutely unsafe prediction, that this Republic would remain an object of wonder and affection, as it had remained through the changes which, during its brief existence, had passed over other countries. We all felt, that however true this might be, it would have been in better taste, it would have shown a more generous and high toned consideration of the feelings of other nations, to omit it; but the circumstances under which it was written, were peculiar, and the lapse was venial. But Mr. Seward was not tempted into telling Mr. Dayton, in Thomson's style, that all other nations would crouch in fear of us, or even regard their own position with dissatisfation on comparing it with ours. That kind of insolent bluster, and the conduct of which it is the exponent, did not come into fashion among folk of any nurture in the old England, until our ancestors had left it. Nor among such people is it tolerated for a moment, here. But "Rule Britannia," is a song written by one of the most eminent and most decorous British poets, and is perhaps higher in favor than any other patriotic British lyric, Campbell's not excepted; and yet I am able to say, that such an arrogant stanza as that quoted above from it, would have insured the instant rejection of a song by the New York National Hymn Committee;—who, by the way, were a fair representation of the general intelligence of the country, only four of the twelve, as was very proper, being taken from men particularly devoted to literature. Another objection would surely have been made to a stanza written in the British poet's style. High literary finish would very properly not have been insisted on; but in America, even a rhyme to "free," for which much will be passed over, is not regarded as a palliation for such an onslaught on the language, as

"The nations not so blest as *thee*."

VI.

But to turn our attention to the songs received by the Committee. No one of them was deemed to satisfy all the requirements of the needed hymn; and so the prize was not awarded.* The decision was,

---

* REPORT OF THE COMMITTEE UPON A NATIONAL HYMN.

The undersigned, having been requested to act as a Committee upon a Prize National Hymn, accepted the office doubtfully, and with some reluctance. They doubted the efficacy of the means proposed to the end which was sought; they were reluctant to assume the function of deciding for their fellow-citizens a question which it seemed to them could really be settled only by general consent and the lapse of time. And deeply as the events of the present momentous period of our country's history stir the heart of every true American, and strong as the tendency appeared among persons in all parts of the land, and of all grades of culture, to give a lyric expression to patriotic feeling, they still felt that the chances were very slight of obtaining at the call of a Committee and by the offer of a prize, a National Hymn which would live in the hearts and upon the lips of the American people. Therefore, although they did not feel at liberty to decline the service asked of them, they expressly reserved to themselves, in their published conditions of competition, "the right of rejecting all contributions, whatever their merit, should none of them be deemed suitable."

The event has fully justified their apprehensions. They received nearly twelve hundred manuscripts in answer to their call, of which about one-third furnished new music as well as words. To the ex-

however, not that all the hymns were devoid of lyric merit. Far from it. The number of those which amination and comparison of these, the Committee addressed themselves at the earliest moment, and gave to the task very much more time than they supposed that they would be called upon to give. Every manuscript received was opened in Committee, read, and duly considered. Every musical composition was performed once; and those found sufficiently meritorious to be worthy of more careful examination were heard in solo and chorus. With comparatively few exceptions, the hymns sent in proved to be of interest only to their writers as rhymed expressions of personal feeling or fancy. Of these exceptions many were excluded from special consideration as being purely devotional, or because they were written either to the national airs of other peoples, or to those in certain vogue with us, the acknowledged insufficiency of which was the reason for the appointment of this Committee. After a careful and repeated consideration of the remainder, the Committee are unanimously of the opinion that, although some of them have a degree of poetic excellence which will probably place them high in public favor as lyrical compositions, no one of them is well suited for a National Hymn. They, therefore, make no award.

Propositions were made for public performances of those hymns which the Committee should think worthy of such distinction; but, upon due consideration, it was deemed most advisable not to accept them. In accordance, however, with one of the conditions of competition, the most meritorious and noticeable of the songs received, have been placed in the hands of publishers (Messrs. RUDD & CARLETON), and will be issued in a volume at their risk; the publication, if profitable, inuring to the benefit of a patriotic fund.

The remaining manuscripts, with their accompanying envelopes (unopened) containing the writers' names, have been destroyed. The money placed at the disposal of the Committee, will be accounted for by their Treasurer to the gentlemen who subscribed it.

The Committee having thus absolved itself of its functions, according to its published conditions of competition, its members beg to inform the various competitors that it no longer exists as a body, and that they, as individuals, have no further power or responsibility upon this subject.

GULIAN C. VERPLANCK,	JOHN A. DIX,
CHARLES KING,	M. H. GRINNELL,
HAMILTON FISH,	LUTHER BRADISH,
GEORGE WM. CURTIS,	RICHARD GRANT WHITE,
J. J. CISCO,	JOHN R. BRODHEAD,
GEORGE T. STRONG,	ARTHUR LEARY,

MAUNSELL B. FIELD.

NEW YORK, *August 9th*, 1861.

were noticeable for poetic excellence, however small in proportion to the multitude that were sent in, was quite as great as could reasonably have been expected, especially when the reluctance of poets of high and long established reputation to enter upon such a competition is considered. Of the winnowings from the immense heaps threshed out of twelve hundred brains, various causes, some of which have been mentioned elsewhere, have left but a few for our examination. But the style and the merits of these are so characteristic, that they offer us, not only their intrinsic beauties, but fine examples in illustration of our theme.

NATIONAL HYMN.

Words and Music by RICHARD STORRS WILLIS.

I.

Anthem of liberty,
  Solemn and grand,
Wake in thy loftiness,
  Sweep through the land!
Light in each breast anew
  Patriot fires,
Pledge the old flag again—
  Flag of our sires!
Fling all thy folds abroad,
  Banner of light!
    Wave, wave forever,
    Flag of our might!
    God for our banner,
    Freedom and Right!
      Amen! Amen!

II.

Spirit of Unity,
  Potent, divine,
Come in thy kindliness,
  All hearts intwine!
Prove to our enemies
  Ever a **rock**,

Ben Marcato.

Anthem of Lib-er-ty, Sol-emn and grand,

Wake in thy lof-ti-ness, Sweep thro' the land!

Light in each breast a-new Pat-ri-ot fires!

And to each traitor-scheme
   Ruinous shock!
Wake the old banner **word!**
   Shout it amain.
      Union forever!
      Once and again!—
      Union forever!
      God it maintain!
         Amen! Amen!

III.

Shades of our forefathers,
   Pass through the land,
Clothed in full majesty,
   Terrible, grand!

Segue Coro.

Fright from their lurking-place,
Treason and wrong,
Wake the old loyalty,
Earnest and strong!
This for our panoply,
What can befal?
Steadfast and loyal,
Naught can appal!
Thus to be loyal
God help us all!
Amen! Amen!

IV

Come, kindly trinity,
Noblest and best,

"Faith, Hope, and Charity,"
  Rule in each breast!
Faith, in our Fatherland,
  Hope, in our Lord,
Charity, still to all
  Blindly who've err'd!
God save the Government!
  Long it defend!
    Thine is the Kingdom,
    Father and Friend!
    Thine be the glory,
    World without end!
        Amen! Amen!

A grand, a truly noble lyric, this. Manly, and

simple, and strong; **full of the** patriot fire which it seeks to light; bold and spirited, and yet tender, brotherly, and imbued with the very soul of Christianity. A song, truly beyond all praise for its motive and its completeness. Having a fine lyric movement, too, and preserving well that medium between simple and figurative utterance of feeling, which allows ornament to lyric poetry without loss of the essential simplicity and directness. The second stanza —so well introduced by the first—sets forth in its invocation the beauty and worth of the Union, with a completeness and convincing force which is the concentration of logic; yet the lyric spirit is never for a moment lost, and it passes, by a transition so natural that it is not noticed, into an outburst of enthusiasm. The third, which summons up the shades of the fathers of the republic, is strongly impressive; the imagination is vivid, the image one of awful dignity and admirable keeping; and the fourth stanza—in which patriotism and Christianity are so inter-penetrated with each other's spirit as to be undistinguishable, and which closes with such a felicitous adaptation of that ascription of praise which, heard at first upon the hilly shores of Galilee, from that time has never ceased to echo through the world— fitly closes this song.*

* I have given this song in short lines according to the author's manuscript. But in fact it is written in verses of four accents, each of which he has broken into two lines.

Anthem of liberty, solemn and grand,
Wake in thy loftiness, sweep through the land!

The music, from the same hand, seems to be born of the words, if indeed it was not twin-born with them. Though its melody is not marked enough to be popular, it has the same character of simplicity, fervor, nobility, and graceful strength by which they are distinguished.

Why, then, is not this song well suited to be our national hymn? Simply because it is not adapted to popular use. Its spirit, except in the first stanza, seems almost too subtle to suit the emotions of large masses of men, who always feel in, so to speak, the most elemental manner; so that words which are written for them or spoken to them should touch strongly and unequivocally those passions which are common to all human creatures. The very imagination, vivid and picturesque, which makes the third stanza of this song so impressive, renders it by so much the less suitable for a national hymn. And another beauty of construction has a like paradoxical effect. It will be seen, on examination of the music, that the last four lines of each stanza, which develope a motive that springs up in the two which precede them, are skilfully made the chorus, and that this chorus is, as it were, an outburst of feeling excited by what has gone before. This is the ideal of chorus singing. The effect is dramatic. We may have our imaginary choruses thus sung, either in our reveries or on the stage; but in practice it will not do. The chorus of a hymn to be sung by a multitude should be the same for every stanza of the song, and should repeat the cardinal lyric motive of the song to the principal musical theme; and in fact be the words and the *tune* by which the song is recognised and spoken of. The announcement here of these critical axioms will enable us to pass over the following songs with brief remark.

The next song has for its central thought the love of liberty—that liberty which is in accordance with truth and right; which love is the strong bond of union between American citizens; and which—never felt, as, indeed, it was never understood, until after the Revolution by which we won our independent national existence—is now the great motive power of the civilized world. The strength of this sentiment is brought out in high relief by contrasting it with the material advantages which coexist with liberty in this country,—a rhetorical device which is not new, but one the force of which long use can never enfeeble. The song, if set to a vigorous, well-marked, pleasing air, could not but become a popular favorite.

OUR NATIVE LAND.

BY JAMES WILLARD MORRIS.

I.

Our Native Land—our Native Land—
    Land dear to every heart!
They breathe free air, they proudly stand,
    Who but of thee have part!
'Tis not broad plains, or skies so clear,
    Or mountains high and grand:
'Tis liberty that makes so dear,
    Our own blest Native Land!

II.

O land beloved—whose Washington
   Toiled nobly for its peace,
Whose patriots bled till life was done,
   That tyranny might cease!
'Twas Freedom's shrine they sought to rear;
   By that we ever stand:
'Tis Liberty that makes so dear
   Our own blest Native Land!

III.

Dear Native Land!—the world's oppressed
   Turn longingly to thee:
Not for thy wealth, thy might confessed,
   Thy noble Unity.
Not for thy wide, embracing sphere,
   Thy sons that waiting stand:
'Tis Liberty that makes so dear,
   Our own blest Native Land!

IV.

Dear Native Land—dear Father Land!
   May peace within thee dwell!
May bounteous life, from God's good hand,
   O'er all thy valleys swell!
May Right and Truth have naught to fear
   While heaven and earth shall stand!
'Tis Liberty that makes so dear
   Our own blest Native Land!

I fancy that I see the captious flout and the ignorant sneer at the assertion made in the remarks precedent to the last song, that the love of a liberty consistent with truth and right was never known until after that liberty was successfully established by the fathers of our Republic. And in fact I have seen Americans talked down to (by British writers, it is almost needless to say, and I am sorry in very deed that it is so), on account of the importance which they regarded the present crisis of their government as possessing to the whole world for all time. These folk I shall send for their answer to Lord Brougham, who, remarking in his "Political Philosophy" (Vol. iii. p. 329) upon the establishment of our national independence, and particularly our adoption of the republican form of government, and the federal plan of constitution, uses the following sufficiently comprehensive language: "This is, perhaps, the most important event in the history of our species." The question whether that government and that constitution shall be perpetuated or destroyed cannot be of much less significance than their original formation:— a fact in which there is no just cause for self-complacency, much less for the assumption of an inflated air of consequence; but which should increase our sense of responsibility, and fix us more firmly in our determination to absolve ourselves with honor of the momentous duties to mankind which the development of our race has laid upon us. The sentiment excited by this look along the path that we have trodden, and that which lies before us, finds a stirring expression in the following noble lyric.*

---

* I regret to say that the envelope containing the name of the author of this song has been lost.

THE NATION'S HYMN.

Our past is bright and grand
   In the purple tints of time;
And the present of our land,
   Points to glories more sublime.
For our destiny is won;
   And 'tis ours to lead the van,
Of the nations marching on,
   Of the moving hosts of man!
      Yes, the Starry Flag alone,
         Shall wave above the van,
      Of the nations sweeping on,
         Of the moving hosts of man!

We are sprung from noble sires,
   As were ever sung in song;
We are bold with Freedom's fires,
   We are rich, and wise, and strong.
On us are freely showered
   The gifts of every clime,
And we're the richest dowered
   Of all the heirs of Time!
      Brothers then, in Union, strong,
         We shall ever lead the van,
      As the nations sweep along,
         To fulfil the hopes of man!

We are brothers; and we know
   That our Union is a tower,
When the fiercest whirlwinds blow,
   And the darkest tempests lower!

We shall sweep the land and sea,
    While we march, in Union, great,
Thirty millions of the free
    With the steady step of fate!
        Brothers then, in Union, strong,
            Let us ever lead the van,
        As the nations sweep along,
            To fulfil the hopes of man!

See our prairies, sky-surrounded!
    See our sunlit mountain chains!
See our waving woods, unbounded,
    And our cities on the plains!
See the oceans kiss our strand,
    Oceans stretched from pole to pole!
See our mighty lakes expand,
    And our giant rivers roll!
        Such a land, and such alone,
            Should be leader of the van,
        As the nations sweep along
            To fulfil the hopes of man!

Yes, the spirit of our land,
    The young giant of the West,
With the waters in his hand,
    With the forests for his crest,—
To our hearts' quick, proud pulsations,
    To our shouts that still increase,
Shall yet lead on the nations,
    To their brotherhood of peace!
        Yes, Columbia, great and strong,
            Shall forever lead the van,
        As the nations sweep along,
            To fulfil the hopes of man!

Too picturesque and fanciful, with all its strength and spirit, for a national hymn, this song has also a serious blemish of excess, if not of assumption, in the second line of the second stanza. A blemish which has its opposite in the following pretty, plaintive, and highly wrought supplication; which seems to have been written not only from the depths of a luxurious humiliation, but with the mistaken notion that a national hymn must necessarily be religious in its character.

A NATIONAL HYMN.

BY J—— S. H——.

O strongest of Helpers! we bring Thee our weakness!
   Oh, tenderest Father! we bring Thee our pain;
Let us cling to Thy feet, till contrition and meekness
   Have won Thee to smile on our country again.

The fairest of lambs in Thy flock of the Nations,
   Has broke the gold tether that bound it to peace;
And only Thy love—not our vain lamentations—
   Can wash off the blood from the snow of its fleece.

Our Eagle, slow-waking from indolent languor,
   Feels a weight on his wings—droops his eye from the sun;
And the wail of his shame, and the scream of his anger,
   Have startled a million brave hearts into one.

To the arms of Thine infinite tenderness take us;
   On Thy neck, lo! the prodigal melts at a touch!
For the sake of our fathers—oh! do not forsake us—
   The children of those whom thou lovedst so much.

Turn not from our pleading, lest blood flow like
    water!
  With the rain of Thy love quench these perilous fires;
That the sweet air, made clean from the scent of the
    slaughter,
  May blush, North and South, with the flag of our
    sires:—

Like a garden of roses and lilies, fresh-blowing,
  Till the dead June seems thus to have blossomed anew;
And Heaven, half in love with the counterfeit growing,
  To have spilled its white stars down in clusters for dew!

Oh, hear us, our God! That the crystal foundations
  Of Liberty's home may be built on a rock;
And Columbia, redeemed—the white lamb of the
    nation,
  Once more may stand fairest and first of the flock.

I return to a suggestion dropped on introducing this song. Hymns were originally sung in honor of some personified quality or idea; and the name may surely be applied now with propriety to a song or ode, in honor of a country, or of the spirit that vivifies a nation. Therefore, the author of the next song might well have given it the name which it bears, even were not the chorus written in a devotional strain. The word 'anthem,' which he uses with perfect admissible poetic licence, is improperly applied to a patriotic national song, as, for instance, in the case of "God Save the King," which is often styled the British National Anthem. But an anthem is essentially ecclesiastical in its form and spirit.

HYMN OF OUR UNION.

BY A. J. H. D.

Oh, the Hymn of our Union! its melody flows
Through the dreams of our children in cradled repose,
When their mothers are singing, our forefathers' songs,
And the voice of their sisters the chorus prolongs;
And the anthem rolls upward in harmonies grand,
To the throne of Jehovah, the strength of our land;

> CHORUS:
> And the Hymn of our Union for ever shall be,
> Jehovah! Jehovah! our strength is in Thee!
> Preserve us, preserve us, united and free;
> Jehovah! Jehovah! our strength is in Thee!

Oh, the Flag of our Union! 'twas woven with light
From the bars of the rainbow, the stars of the night!
In the vesture of Freedom it swept from on high,
And its hues are all blended with beams of the sky.
'Twas the blood of our martyrs that crimson'd its bars,
And the souls of our heroes shine out from its stars!

> CHORUS:
> And the Hymn of our Union for ever shall be, &c.

Oh, the Land of our Union! it sweetens the morn
With the fragrance of orchards, the sunshine of corn:
In its bountiful bosom the fountains are sure,
And the gold of its furrows is wealth for the poor:
And the children of exile as kindred may toil
In the vineyards of freedom, with sons of the soil.

> CHORUS:
> And the Hymn of our Union for ever shall be, &c.

Oh, the Soul of our Union! it blossomed of old,
With the pray'rs of the loyal, the faith of the bold;
And the fruits of its harvest we garner anew
In the deeds of the valiant, the lives of the true:
For the seeds of all Freedom in union are sown,
And the hopes of all nations are twined with our own.

CHORUS:

And the Hymn of our Union for ever shall be, &c.

The next song, although not at all suited to be a national hymn, is one which no American can read without a glow of interest. The graves of our dead heroes and statesmen are a living bond between us which it would take generations of alienated political existence to break. This thought is skilfully elaborated by the author of the following stanzas.

OUR FATHERS' GRAVES.

BY CHARLES FARNHAM.

I.

From Oregon's eternal hills,
 From California's golden shore,
From northern plains, whose thousand rills
 Unite to swell the cataract's roar—
March on, march on in stern array
 From all along Atlantic's waves!
Shall tyrant despots hold their sway
 Around our fathers' sacred graves?

II.

Beneath the golden eagle's wings
  That banner proud is waving on,
Where every land its offering flings
  Upon the grave of Jefferson;
Where Patrick Henry's soul of fire
  Still burns amid disunion's woes,
And Randolph's voice shall not expire
  Amid Virginia's sacred groves.

III.

That land is ours—that beauteous land
  Where Marion and Sumpter rest;
And Jackson's tomb—Oh, let it stand
  To guard the gateway of the West!
Preserve the grave of Washington—
  His land—his name—his home, is ours!
To Vernon's mount, march on, march on,
  And strew your Father's grave with flowers.

IV.

Let Webster's voice each bosom warm,
  And Clay the patriot's soul inspire,
And Benton's spirit guide the storm
  When Freedom's dauntless sons expire!
And till the love of Truth shall fall,
  And sink amid corruption's waves,
The Stars and Stripes shall float o'er all,
  O'er all our Fathers' sacred graves.

"E PLURIBUS UNUM."

BY THE REV. JOHN PIERPONT.

Air—" *The Star-Spangled Banner.*"

I.

The harp of the minstrel with mélody rings,
   When the Muses have taught him to touch and to tune it;
And although it may have a full octave of strings,
   To both maker and minstrel the harp is a unit.
      So, the power that creates
      Our Republic of States,
   To harmony tunes them at different dates;
And, many or few, when the Union is done,
Be they thirteen or thirty, the nation is one.

II.

The science that measures and numbers the spheres,
   And has done so since first the Chaldean began it,
Now and then, as she counts them, and measures their years,
   Brings into our system and names a new planet.
      Yet the old and new stars,
      Venus, Neptune, and Mars,
   As they drive round the sun their invisible cars,
Whether faster or slower their races are run,
Are " E Pluribus Unum "—of many made one.

III.

Of those federate spheres, should but one fly the track,
   Or with others conspire for a general dispersion,
By the great central orb they would all be brought back,
   And held, each in its place, by a wholesome " coercion."

Were one daughter of light
Indulged in her flight,
They might all be engulphed by old Chaös and night;
So must none of our sisters be suffered to run,
For, "E Pluribus Unum"—We all go, if one.

IV.

Let the Demon of discord our melody mar,
   Or Treason's red hand rend our system asunder,
Break one string from our harp, or extinguish one star,
   The whole system's ablaze with its lightning and thunder.
      Let that discord be hushed!
      Let the traitors be crushed,
   Though "Legion" their name, all with victory flushed;
For aye must our motto stand, fronting the sun,
"E Pluribus Unum"—The many are one.

This most ingenious and fanciful composition is quite perfect in its kind, and will add a bright and ever green leaf to the wreath of one of our veteran and most highly esteemed poets. Commencing at a point remote from its subject, it compels the very laws of harmony and gravitation into the service of patriotism. The ingenuity with which this is done makes the reading of the poem a succession of pleasing surprises, each surpassing the other, till they culminate in the last lines of the last stanza. But in spite of this artful contrivance, nay, by very reason of it, the brilliancy of the song, like the blaze of a beacon, is a warning to those who would be attracted by its light. For with all its intrinsic excellence, it is ill adapted to music, and is a model of what a song intended for a national hymn ought not to be.

At the request of a lady who rescued it from the buck-basket hereinbefore mentioned, I give the following song,—placing it here because its simplicity and manifest intentional adaptation to mere vocal purposes, contrast strongly with the style of the one last given. It had no title; and the envelope containing the name of its author was not recovered.

I.

Flag of freemen gone before us,
While thy starry folds float o'er us,
    All the land, from sea to sea,
    Now and ever shall be free.
Mindful of our fathers' story,
Mindful of our country's glory,
    Be our care from age to age,
    Well to keep that heritage.

Chorus. Flag of freemen gone before us
    While thy starry folds float o'er us,
        All the land, from sea to sea,
        Now and ever shall be free.

II.

Heroes lived and died to gain it.
Living, dying we'll maintain it.
    For this land from sea to sea,
    Freemen's arms shall e'er keep free.

Freemen born of every nation,
Freemen born in every station,
    Heart and hand for this shall plight,
    Gathering here in freedom's might.

Chorus. Flag of freemen, &c.

III.

Bold alone, united bolder,
Millions shoulder stand to shoulder,
    Stretching on from sea to sea
    In the Union of the free.
We that Union swear to cherish,
May its foes forever perish!
    Let it glorious and strong,
    Shield the right and crush the wrong.

Chorus. Flag of freemen, &c.

IV.

Truth shall govern, honor fire us;
Loyal liberty inspire us!
    Not in vain the world shall see
    God has made this people free.
May he guide, and may he guard us;
May his blessing e'er reward us:
    So shall the Republic stand,
    Peace and plenty crown the land.

Chorus. Flag of freemen gone before us,
    While thy starry folds float o'er us,
        All the land, from sea to sea,
        Now and ever shall be free.

GOD SAVE OUR FATHERLAND.

BY REV. JOHN H. HOPKINS.

I.

God save our Fatherland, from shore to shore!
God save our Fatherland, one evermore!
   No hand shall peril it,
   No strife shall sever it,
East, West, North, and South;
One evermore!

    Chorus. God save our Fatherland, true home of freedom!
    God save our Fatherland, One evermore.
    One in her hills and streams,
    One in her glorious dreams,
    One in love's noblest themes!
    One evermore!

MUSIC BY C. JEROME HOPKINS.

II.

Strong in the hearts of men, love is thy throne!
Union and Liberty crown thee alone!
    Nations have sighed for thee!
    Our sires **have** died for thee!
We all are **true** to thee.
All are thine **own**!

    Chorus. God save our Fatherland, blest home of
        Freedom!
      God save our Fatherland, **One evermore.**
        One in **her** hills and streams,
        One in her glorious dreams,
        One in love's noblest themes!
        One evermore!

III.

Ride on, proud ship of state, tho' tempests low'r,
Ride on in majesty, glorious in pow'r.
    Tho' fierce the blast may be,
    No blast shall shatter thee;
    Storms shall but bring to thee
      Sunshine once more.

Chorus. God save our Fatherland, blest home of Freedom!
God save our Fatherland, One evermore.
    One in her hills and streams,
    One in her glorious dreams,
    One in love's noblest themes!
      One evermore!

These words seem to have been written, merely as the vehicle of the music which accompanies them. Yet they are nervous, spirited, warm with the fire of patriotism, and have a fine, manly rhythm. The music stands in the first rank of its class. The simplicity of its motive, and the strength and symmetry of the whole composition give it a noble beauty. It is in the highest style of plain choral writing; and the feeling which it inspires, no less than the purity with which it is written, make it a work of which no composer need be ashamed.

Why then not accept it as a national hymn? Because, simple as it is, for the public at large it is absolutely unsingable. People generally would be puzzled to discover its melody, much more to retain

it. They would say that it had no *tune*. These objections apply, too, with peculiar force to the chorus, that part of a national hymn which should be least obnoxious to them. The melody of the chorus is different from that of the solo part, and it is based upon modulation; a radical objection which, of course, applies equally to the harmonies. In the chorus of a national hymn, the harmony should be confined to the three primary chords, with, perhaps, the rare addition of the seventh. Upon these harmonies can be based all the effects desirable for such a song. But there is yet another, and a more essential objection to this music as that of a national hymn, an objection which does not in the least touch its intrinsic beauty, which has to do with the kind, not the degree, of its

excellence. With all its strength and dignity, it is not confident; and a national hymn should be, above all things, confident in tone, though not aggressive. Its office is to cheer and to inspire. But the spirit of this melody is prayerful, tearful. True, its supplication is majestic, its grief is noble. So might Moses, hope-bereft, have implored upon the lonely top of Pisgah: so might the stricken Peter have wept in the outer court of Caiphas. But if it fitly uttered the woes of the whole hierarchy of prophets, and the aspirations of all the archangels, it would be none the less unfitted for the use of a nation of determined men.

The next song is merely a direct and fervent rhythmical utterance of the sentiments and aspirations

which fill the heart of every patriot when he turns his thoughts upon his country. And this is just what a national hymn for our people should be. Nothing is lacking to such a song as this but that great lack, the music that will give it voice and win it universal favor.*

NATIONAL HYMN.

BY J. HILTON JONES.

I.

Great God, all just, all wise!
On whom our trust relies,
To Thee our nation cries,
    God save the land!
Charge it with patriot fire,
Guard it from faction dire,
And from rebellion's ire
    God save the land!

Chorus. Charge it with patriot fire, &c.

---

* I add here the music of a song received by the committee the melody of which, though unsuited to a national hymn, is purely vocal, of an elegant symmetry and enchanting sweetness. Its author has evidently been an admiring student of Mozart; but he has given us no imitation of him except a reminiscence of "*Vedrai carino*" in the bass of the first strain. There is a striking similarity, extending to the harmony and movement of inner parts, between the third strain of this composition and the fifth of Mr. Willis's. Is it an unconscious reminiscence by both composers which their critic is unable to trace.

NATIONAL HYMNS.

II.

Bless it with plenty's smile!
Cheer it with honest toil!
Make all its foes recoil!
    God save the land!
Crown it with Truth and Right!
O'er it shed Virtue's light,
Honor and Glory bright!
    God save the land!
Chorus. Crown it with Truth and Right, &c.

III.

Garlands of Hope entwine,
With Faith and Love divine,
O'er blessed Freedom's shrine!
    God save the land!

BY J. R. THOMAS.

Great God, all just, all wise,
On whom our strength relies,
To Thee our nation cries,
 God save the land!

Chorus. Great God, all just, all wise, &c.

Among the songs received were some which contained a single stanza or two of remarkable merit; and of these, one in the form of an apostrophe to "Our National Ensign" ended with the following noble lines, in which a large and stirring thought is well developed and sustained, and brought to a fine climax, with, however, a slight and easily remedied defect of metaphor in the fifth line.

"Flag of two ocean shores!
  Whose everlasting thunder roars
From deep to deep in storm and foam!—
  Though with the sun's red set
  Thou sink'st to slumber, yet
  With him in glory great
Thou risest, and shalt share his tomb!
  Thou banner beautiful and grand,
  Float thou forever o'er our land!"

Another called "A Hymn for Freedom," opens with the following spirited stanza:

"A hymn for Freedom! let it ring
  As far as earth and time;

>   And choral as the grandest lays
>   That made the stars sublime.
>   Raise high the strain from land to land,
>   Till sea shall sound to sea;
>   And all Earth's voices shall prolong
>   The anthem of the free!"

This promises well; but the remainder is unequal to it, and falls, as was the case in many other instances, into the making of protests against kings and lords, and assurances of security from despots and tyrants! For us these things belong to a past world, from which we are cut off by a gulf as impassable as that between Lazarus and Dives. It were as well to assure us that we are safe from giants and griffins.

These songs are few in number to bring forward as specimens of the best that could be found in nearly twelve hundred. It should, however, be remembered that they are only about half of those that were laid aside for publication. But the lyric merit of several of these is such that the country may accept them with pleasure as patriotic offerings. The tone of all of them, with a single exception, is healthy and manly; and indeed it is remarkable, and an indication of the most favorable kind as to our national character, that among this great mass of verse, written in the always somewhat overweening spirit of patriotism, and a great part of which was produced by some of the most unlettered, uncultured people in the country, there was no appreciable exhibition of any other than a spirit of magnanimity, and of Christian charity. The sins against good taste in a literary point of view were numberless; many of the songs being in this respect only one monstrous crime in four acts, being four stanzas. But of offences against that higher taste which dictates a scrupulous respect for the personality, and a consideration for the feelings of others, whether individuals or nations, there were, to all intents and purposes, none whatever. Arrogant self-assertion did not appear; though firm determination, high hope, and consciousness of grave responsibility were constantly exhibited. Aspirations for the success of Truth and Right were the burden, or the climax, of a very large majority of the songs. To have been the means of eliciting such an unconscious exhibition of national high-mindedness is a sufficient reward to the committee, although their efforts were unsuccessful upon the point to which they were directed. In truth, this manifestation is worth infinitely more than the unwritten ideal national hymn in the hope of eliciting which the committee was appointed.

VII.

It has been already said that the large majority of the songs received by the committee were the merest common-place, brief effusions of decent dulness, or fantastic folly. But it would have been strange indeed if among the contributions of such a great number of competitors, scattered over the whole country, there were not some traits of originality possessing a certain interest, though it were not exactly of that kind that properly pertains to a national hymn. Not a few of the manuscripts tended much to relieve the tedium of the readings by their revelations of the very peculiar notions entertained by their writers as to the kind of words and music suited to a national hymn, and some of them by the complacent requests which accompanied them. The following composition was one of the earliest opened.

A NATIONAL HYMN.

All hail our country great,
May she never falter;

But every darned Secessionist
Be hung up by a halter!

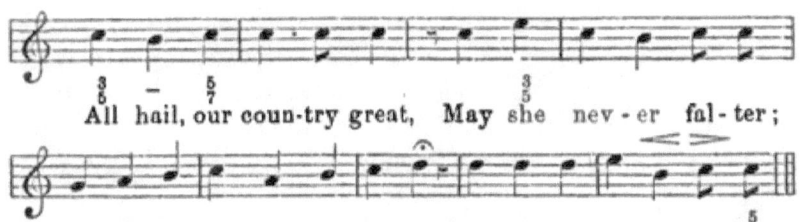

All hail, our coun-try great, May she nev-er fal-ter;

But every damn'd seces-sion-ist Be hung up by the hal-ter.

(Appended by the *author of the verses*.)

It is supposed the committee understand fugue and figured bass. The money may be sent to the author at Albany.

It may, perhaps, be doubted whether the author of the above was quite serious; but of the sober thriftiness of purpose with which the mass of the committee's correspondents wrote, there can be no question whatever. One, who inhabits New England, sent a song entitled "The Nation's Bride," which he positively refuses to give to the public for less than the prize offered—two hundred and fifty dollars; and of which therefore, it can only be said here, that after bringing a mysterious person, called the nation's bride, upon the carpet in the first stanza, he says in the second:—

>   And lo here is the sidesaddle
>   Which the bride with horse and bridle
>   May at her pleasure take a ride
>   In the buoyancy of her pride.

As to this performance—the song, not the ride—the author makes the following communication:—

The foregoing hymn was in part written by me after seeing a lady on horsback which in my fancy resembled Washington in feature and exsspression of face, which hymn since seeing the reward offord for a national hymn with some addition and allteration to suit the occasion I send to your committee for considderation for the foregoing object and prize the only inducement being our nations glory and the need of the monney offerd. As I am no musician I shell not attempt to compose the music.

This confession of mixed motives, though it may show less tact, is probably the fruit of more candor than appears in some other letters written by competitors; and the writer's refraining from the composition of the music, simply because he was not a musician, shows a capacity of self-knowledge which does not always accompany greater advantages and greater pretensions than his. He certainly was not of kin to the Irishman who didn't know whether he could play the violin, because he had "niver thried." It is safe to say that if all the people who were no musicians had refrained from writing music for a national hymn, the committee's labors would have been considerably shortened.

It might have been well, too, if a distinct and uniform notion of what a national hymn is had been impressed upon the general mind of the nation before twelve hundred individuals of it attacked thirteen hapless committee-men upon that subject, pen in hand. For instance, one competitor sent in the Declaration of Independence in rhyme, after this fashion:—

When in the course of human events, a people needful find
They must dissolve the bonds that did them to another bind,

And to assume, 'mongst earthly powers, a separate, equal station,
To which by law they entitled are, as well as by creation;
In such events, respect demands that they should then declare
The reasons that impell'd the change, and what the causes are.
We (the Americans) hold these, as truths self-evident,
That men created equal are, when on this earth they're sent,
With rights inalienable endow'd, as liberty and life!
Pursuit of happiness as well (within this world of strife).

And so on, for a hundred lines. Another sent a composition of fourteen stanzas, of which the following are specimens:—

A CONSTITUTION HYMN.

What is that stings the Eare?—it sounds as of yore
Is the Nation a Bleeding—by the Cannon once more
Some links seeme severd—From the Union's Throng
The Banner says stay—To the Union Belong

Corus—Then all hail, Constitution—Thy Sperit we'll Keep
    For thy starspangled banner—it never shall sleep

The Old Constitution—is seald to each Heart,
So firm by the Fathers—no Orater can start
All hale to Columbia—for the Trater must fall
For Linkon's deep measures—must silence them all

Corus—Then all Hale Constitution—Thy sperit we'll Keep
    For thy starspangled Banner—it never will sleep

As Chaneless our sperits—and Fredom as Time
And the starspangled banner—ever wave in the line
And the sperit for fredom—will not ceace to run
For he that wild fredom was grate Washington

Corus—Then all hale Constitution—thy sperit we'll keep
    For thy starspangled Banner—it never will sleep

Heres the last dying words—From a Sogers bold Toung
That the Stares and the Stripes—in Union be sung
Equal Rights and Fredom—is the old mottoes demand
In the old seventysix spirit—our nation shall Stand

Corus—Then all hail Constitution—thy Sperit we'll keep
For thy starspangled banner—it never will sleep

God's willd free to man—all things thatt he needes
From his Birth to his grave—while onward he speedes
Yet peace fredom and union—the best boon to life
Except what god made—when he made man a wife

Then shout for such union—the best boon thats given
It gladens the heart—and wills us for heaven

From another came a sort of chronicle dallad, longer by half than "Chevy Chace," which opened thus:—

FOR THE NATION A CHRONICLE.

O land of America of the i sing
   As prophetic visions oer the Rise
Thou Boasted land without a king
   Thy Glory granted from the skies

From poperys plagues thy children were
   Among heathen driven to find a home
And the pilgrim fathers to God did swear
   That popery among them should not come

Skipping over thirty-four stanzas, we read the following record of the state of affairs at the time of the writing of the chronicle. The South is,—

Proclaiming war against the north
    Because they Could not Rule them there
Swearing fire and Sword they will Bring forth
    And lay their towns and cities Bare

These States Confederate are they say
    With a Constitution and a flag
Davis as President there Bears sway
    With his Beauregard & Col. Brag

Now our president north A. Lincoln is
    With Scot and Seward as Counsellors
Calls all honest men now to Be his
    To put down this Band of conspirators

The word goes out the north arise, &c.

Yet another sends—

THE HYMN OF OUR COUNTRY.

TUNE—*Kate Kearney.* CHORUS—*A Southerly Wind.*

GREAT FOUNTAIN OF LIGHT! GREAT LIFE-GIVING POWER!
THINE ALL-SEEING EYE is a CONSUMING FIRE!
That moves us to Live! that moves us to Die!
That raises our Spirits to Endless Joy!
    Hail! LIGHT of LIFE! Hail! SPIRIT of FORCE!
    That LIGHT which at first created all things,
    That LIGHT in man is the IMAGE of SOURCE,
    That LIGHT of dominion o'er Earth's offsprings.
That LIGHT which led the Israelites,
That LIGHT which glowed on Sinai's Mount,
That LIGHT which brought Good Tidings Rites,
That LIGHT with the Dove at Holy Font.

That Light the Power to live and move,
That Light from Heaven that blinded Saul,
That Light which leaves its earthy shell,
That Light which frees th' Immortal Soul.
That Light doth invest in Raiments of White,
That Light doth illumine the Mansions Above,
That Light of the Living and not of the dead,
Is the Light of all Worlds and Souls of Love.

  Chorus.—A Fatherly Voice, and a Godly Eye,
   Are the Life and Light now raising
   The "Land of Flowers" to greet the Sky,
   The Freemen and Daughters to praising.
    Away with the troubles of Earth!
    Away with the sins of the Nation!
    Huzza! for America's Chief!
    The Rulers! and Laws of the Union!
     Hark! Hark!! Forward!!!
     Hozanna! Hozanna!! Hozanna!!!
     Hark! Hark!! Forward!!!
     The Star Spangled Banner!
     Hark! Hark!! Forward!!!
     Hozanna! Hozanna!! Hozanna!!!
     Hark! Hark!! Forward!!!
     God Save the Union!

The foregoing lines form about one-third of this national hymn, which, by the way, it will be seen, is directed to be sung, the body of it to "Kate Kearney," and the Chorus to "A Southerly Wind and a Cloudy Sky." Will any gentleman or lady please to favor the company in which he or she reads these pages, with the first four lines of the Song and the Chorus respectively, singing them to those airs. And in regard to the airs, and consequently the rhythm, which some writers thought suitable, the following examples are interesting :—

NATIONAL HYMN.

TUNE—"*Coming through the Rye,*" or any S. M.

Of Freedom's flag with its unfledgd bird,
   That broke the British Spars,
And Lions teeth, the world has heard,
   Though it had but thirteen stars.

Chorus—Lo in this dark mysterious hour,
   The flag of the brave and free
Brought to the dust by brutal power,
   Too blind the right to see.

*   *   *   *   *   *   *

The Despots Reign is short indeed,
   O'er mortals on the Earth,
When Tyrants swing or the Eagles sing
   Of freedoms second birth.

Chorus—A second birth ! a strange idea,
   When Demons hold the Reins,
And mortals live in slavish fear
   On gross material planes.

UNION FOREVER.

MUSIC—*Come haste to the* Wedding, or *Rural Felicity.*

Our nation's in trouble, and what is the reason
   That this fruitful land is so drench'd with our gore?
There's fighting, and murder, and high-handed treason,
   And all for the purpose to strengthen slave power.

The Union forever, no traitor may sever,
   Or cause our brave flag to be laid in the dust,
Freedom, our natural inheritance,
   Sanctioned by Heaven, we know to be just.

II.

The labourers, the noble, that furnish our living,
   And all other comforts this earth can produce;
And there is no good reason for our believing
   That one man was made for another man's use.

   The Union forever, no traitor may sever,
      Or cause our brave flag to be laid in the dust,
   Freedom, our natural inheritance,
      Sanctioned by Heaven, we know to be just.

NATIONAL HYMN.

Tune—*Lord Lovel.*

Great source of light, Eternal One, the Infinite, the real,
Where wisdom reigns thy will is done, all else is but ideal,
   Ideal, all else is but ideal.

While we in*fi*nite laws survey, all finite things depart,
But where mankind on mortals prey, there's no law on the heart,
   Heart, heart, there's no law on the heart.

In seventy-six, our unfledged bird made Briton's symbol groan
Lo, how the hearts of men were stirred when the nestling shook the throne,
   Throne, throne, when the nestling shook the throne.

Behold its talons, now how strong, a mighty power on earth,
Hark, hear its thrilling native song, of freedom's second birth,
   Birth, birth, of freedom's second birth.

A second birth!! hold on dear bird, freedom lives forever,
Allied to God, the living Word, it was a mortal never,
    Never, it was a mortal never.

Hence to the individual man, and to his God we look
For wisdom now to lead the van, till despotism is shook,
    Shook, shook, till despotism is shook.

Lo, while there's a tempestuous sea, and mind and matter fighting,
We fain would put our trust in Thee, who in the dust was writing,
    Writing, who in the dust was writing.

   *   *   *   *   *   *   *

To thy Almighty power we look, to save this youthful nation,
Inspire us from thy living book, that has no final station,
    Station, that has no final station.

   *   *   *   *   *   *   *

Let artificial swords and spears be subject to the pen,
And all be subject to ideas, till seraphs cry amen,
    Amen, till seraphs cry amen.

It will be observed, that a due regard for the dimensions to which this volume must be restricted, has made an excision of some of the stanzas of this hymn necessary; for it more than rivalled in length the dolorous ballad to the tune of which it was written. Only those who can sing the hymn to the tune of "Lord Lovel," or have the privilege of hearing it sung, can realize what a very striking effect the author has attained even in his very first stanza.

A rhythmical effect, somewhat similar to that of the foregoing song, has been attained by the writer of that from which the following stanzas are quoted. In the choice of his subject he passes by the flag, the **union, and** even liberty, **in favor** of that upon which he—very justly—believes that the safety **of all of** them depends.

THE BALLOT-BOX.

Our country, our country! the Palm and the Pine,
Lake, River, and Delta, Rock, Prairie, and Vine!
From Ocean to ocean thy banner doth float!
How broad is the Realm that we rule by the vote!
  By a vote, vote, omnipotent vote!
  What destinies hang on the Freeman's vote!

Our bold mountain Eagle flies fearless and far,
Bearing home on his pinions new Star after Star,
Till the Old Thirteen have become thirty-four!
And our "STAR-SPANGLED BANNER" hath room for no more!
  By a vote, vote, omnipotent vote!
  What destinies hang on the Freeman's vote!

Though we join hand in hand with the Genius of Toil,
We turn from the health-giving, wealth-giving soil,
From carrying our fortunes with Energy's Hand,
To the holier duty of ruling the land,
  By a vote, vote, omnipotent vote!
  What destinies hang on the Freeman's vote!

  * * * * * *

Then ho for the Ballot-Box! Still shall it be
The Bane of the Tyrant, the Boon of the Free!
And the old Stars and Stripes shall evermore float,
O'er the Land of our Love, that we rule by a VOTE!
  By a vote, vote, omnipotent vote!
  What destinies hang on the Freeman's vote!

The doubts expressed by the writer of the following note and the song which accompanied it, are of the most distracting nature. The committee had no thought that they were about to place any one in such distressing uncertainty.

Gentlemen: **I have** hesitated, or halted, between *three* opinions, in relation to the National Hymn, whether to write of the nation as it was, or as it is, or as it **is to be.** If you think the following lines worth publishing, **please do so.**

    While **men their brothers' blood are spilling,**
    The muses seem to **be unwilling**
To sing a strain about the nation complimentary **at all,**
    While there is such an envious feeling,
    Or one is from the other stealing.

        CHORUS.

Or while the Constitution's reeling as Adam's did before the fall,
Whose pen will be inspired to write a song to satisfy the call?

The first line of this chorus presents a difficulty, and one which touches the origin and the antiquity of the Constitution of the United States. We have heard of the Spanish hidalgo whose faith in the antiquity of his blood was such that he had a picture painted of Noah entering the ark with a package under his arm, labelled " Papers relating to the —— family ;" but we are nevertheless startled to learn that the principles of our Constitution are so antediluvian that it can be likened to Adam's. The difficulty may, however, be partially solved by Dr. Brandreth's triumphant answer to the searching question, " What is the constitution?" *i. e.* " That which constitutes."

Clearly, therefore, Adam's constitution, and the Constitution of the United States are similar, and in one point identical. But that Adam's constitution was reeling before the fall, is a new revelation. We all knew that he ate the apple; but none of us had hitherto suspected that the consequence was a case for diet and medicine. But not to be led into wild and distracting speculation, leading on the one hand to "fate, free-will, fore-knowledge absolute," and on the other to pills and impaired digestion, we must deny ourselves further extracts from this song; and turn to the following not uninteresting examples of a peculiar style of national hymn writing.

FREEDOM'S JUBILEE.

Come nations, kingdoms, people, climes,
Inspire the muse, indite the rhymes.
Let voice and sound and hearts unfurl,
And roll an anthem round the world.
   'Tis Freedom's Jubilee,—hurrah!

Come babes and wise and ancients grim,
With slaves and cripples all fall in,
Tune up your pipes, and trim your lights,
Swell, swell the chorus, vales and heights.
   'Tis Freedom's Jubilee,—hurrah!

Come kings and princes, priest and sage;—
Reject your pomp—fear not to engage.
The car of freedom cannot wait;
So get aboard and leave your state.
   'Tis Freedom's Jubilee,—hurrah!

   *   *   *   *   *   *

Come Lords and Ladies, old and young,
The song of freedom must be sung.
Now toe the mark—don't make wry faces,
Though some may not have all the graces.
    'Tis Freedom's Jubilee,—hurrah!

Come black and white, and red and yellow;
Now sing like locusts till you're hollow.
Aristocrats only 'xcused from singing,
But they can set their servants grinning.
    'Tis Freedom's Jubilee,—hurrah!

The orchestra down, from Master Jubal
To Doctor Franklin's penny whistle;
And all the vocal songs of nations
Reverberate around Creation.
    'Tis Freedom's Jubilee,—hurrah!

THE SNUG LITTLE FARM IN THE WEST.

There's a snug little homestead well known in the West,
  But the owner has pass'd like the snow.
JOHN REDSKIN, the hunter, and all have confest
  It was time he had gone long ago.

Chorus.
Its name 'tis in vain to disguise,
    For of farms 'tis the pink and the queen;
And I see from the smile in your eyes
    That you guess the old homestead I mean.

DON PEDRO from Madrid came posting in haste,
  And the gold he took from it in store,
But his mining was rough, so he drove it to waste,
  And the rule of the Don is no more.

    Its name &c.

Then Wouter van Twiller came waddling around;
    In the "*Swamp*" for the dollars he dips,
But back he has gone to his own muddy ground,
    And his Schiedam in Holland he sips.

       Its name &c.

Then Monsieur Crapeau came along with a hop,
    And he show'd us some feats with his toes,
But the frost was severe, and he vowed not to stop,
    He had such a regard for his nose.

       Its name &c.

Johnny Bull followed next, and he thought it would suit,
    For a pretty close farmer was he,
And the garden might still have been bearing him fruit
    But he foolishly sow'd it with—*tea*.

       Its name &c.

Now the homestead is clear'd and the acres are ours;
    See our Sammy the rich meadow delves;
And for sake of the blood that has water'd its flowers
    We'll keep it, I think, for ourselves.

       Its name &c.

The following compositions failed to obtain the prize, it will be seen, because of their violation of the condition announced, that the hymn must be adapted to the whole country, and not be appropriate to the present moment, only.

NATIONAL HYMN.

TUNE—*The Old Granet State.*

What has caused this great commotion
Through our land and through our Ocean,
Tis Jeff. Davis and his boasting
Band of secession men;
We would like to give him powder,
We would like to give him powder,
We would like to give him powder
And blow him out the land.

* * * * * *

Come all blooming blushing maidens
Make our hearts to swell with singing
While we hear your voices ringing
On our march to southern lands;
Yes we know you'd swell the chorus,
Yes we know you'd swell the chorus,
Yes we know you'd swell the chorus
For your noble country men.

1861.

TUNE—*Old Dan Tucker.*

1.

With stars and stripes and martial glee,
We'll send Jeff. Davis up a tree;
His trait'rous band must follow suit
Because they like that kind of fruit.

Chorus. Get out of the way old Jeff. Davis,
Out the way old Jeff. Davis,
Out the way old Jeff. Davis,
You're to late to come to enslave us.

* * * * * *

5.

You've got John Canvin (or Calvin) on your side,
To show that God is satisfied,
With Slavery's vile adulterous shame,
And in your prayers invoke his name.

Chorus. Get out of the way old Jeff. Davis,

6.

But we have Jesus, as you see,
Who says the captive shall be free,
We know his counsels must prevail;
Almighty wisdom cannot fail.

Chorus. Get out of the way old Jeff. Davis.

5th and 6th verses not to be sung: they are intended only for the clergy.

June 1th. M——TOWN.

Gentlemen, this is My Himn for Your Advertisement In the Dollar Paper for the 20th of June it might answer for the Verry Himn You Want if this should Happen to do the Porpose i will then do some more for you and if this will answer you will of course do according to Contract and if it should be to Simple it is not more lost then 3cts I will now State the Effects of the himn. One night I dreamed that I did See, the Southarns ships where On the Sea, the Union men where not affraid, this tune the band So Sweetely Played, In the Morning When I did Wake, to fight for the Union My Heart did Ache, My Wife so Cried and beged all day, that I with Her at Home should Stay, I then did say it would be best, if I would Share my life with the Rest, I Have a brother thats dear to my Heart, he is now in war we hat to Part, President Lincoln He doth reign, and he will bring the South to Shame, Jeneral Scott is wide awake Southarns cant Him Overtake, Jeffarson Davis Should be Hung, In Spite of all that He Has don, Kind Readers when you Sing this Song, I Hope my Brother will be along, this is all I do Compose i l Bring my Poetry to a close, Address thus

Penna.

A PATRIOTIC HYMN.

8, 8, 6.   CHARING, AITHLOME.

I.
Our government in days of yore,
Of States thirteen—now thirty-four—
    In union firmly stood;
And shall division now be sought,
Of this fair land so dearly bought,
    With our forefathers' blood?

II.
Forbid it Lord,—nay rather let,
The rebels who would so forget,
    Their solemn oaths and vows,
Receive the punishment condign,
By fetters, halters, grape shot, fine,
    Or what the law allows.

III.
O treason, treason, treason, O!
Most awful crime on earth we know,
    Our country to betray!
Yet if the rebels will repent
And pray that pardon may be sent,
    To sinners great as they,—

*   *   *   *   *

V.
Our government as 'twas design'd—
Republican, of fed'ral kind—
    We magnify and prize;
Secession (or by other name
Rebelion), which the traitors claim,
    We will not recognise.

The last song **exhibits yet** another imitation of Thomson. The line, "O treason, treason, treason, O!" is too plainly copied from that in Thomson's "Sophonisba":—

O! Sophonisba, Sophonisba, O!

which some literary énemy, or friend, of the author thus profanely travestied;—

"O! **Jemmy** Thomson, Jemmy Thomson, O!"

But if **imitation** must be stigmatized, or at **least** pointed out, what is to be said of the following verses which **are** without signature **or date?** Did the writer intend **an imposition, or was** the **author** of Brahma really **an unconfessed competitor for the prize?**

UNION.

I.

Individual several, indisintegrative whole!
Corporeal nationality, national soul!
Matter indistinguishable, immaterial seen!
End of all means, of all ends mean!

 Chorus—Thus with eye unfilmed we see
   All the charms of unity;
   Clearly thus have comprehended,
   What our forefathers intended.

II.

Of sempiternal potency, preëxistent power!
Sweet of our bitter, of our sweetness sour!
Of Buncombe progenitor, issue of old Ops,
Live thou upon thy Buncombe, die he within thy chops!

 Chorus—Thus with eye unfilmed, &c.

III.

Infissiparous symbol of politic etern,
Securing Uncle Sam what's hisn and every State what's
   hern,
Of strength redintegrative, of pulchritude e'er fresh,
Secesh were not without thee, and with thee no secesh!

Chorus—Thus with eye unfilmed we see.

IV.

Thus, end of thy beginning, beginning of thy end,
Ample power to break bestowing, reserving power to
   mend,
Self destroyer, self-producer, thou hast pluck and strength
   enough
To cuff well all thy enemies, were thy enemy not Cuff.

Chorus—Thus with eye unfilmed we see
   All the charms of unity;
   Clearly thus have comprehended,
   What our forefathers intended.

But what need of imitation? Had Anna Matilda, or Laura Maria, or any other of the contributors to "The World" risen from their graves, nay had the Rosa Matilda of the Rejected Addresses and Pope's Person of Quality appeared with them, could they have produced anything which they would have owned more gladly than the following compositions.*

---

* The late "World" newspaper of New York is of course not referred to; but its namesake, which was published in London towards the close of the last century, and in which the Della Cruscan poetry appeared.

AMERICA.

America, our lovely nation,
Offspring of th' eternal day,
Why should not the whole creation
Homage to thy virtues pay?
Now in the field in heat of battle,
On the deep where cannons roar,
Firm united and undaunted
Banish tyrants from your shore!

Long has liberty laid sleeping,
Wrapt in darkness, bound in chains,
The nation independance seeking,
Rouse to arms your rights regain.
High exalted rode the eagle,
Glorious as the morning star.
Nature smiles and seems delighted,
Freedom's voice is heard afar.

Liberty thou here shalt flourish
On the soil that gave thee birth.
All your sons your rights shall nourish,
Blest with festive joy and mirth.
While the nations of the world.
Tot'ring, shiv'ring in despair,
Mourn their organizeing victims,
Cries of death ascend the air

Long live the constitution!
Long live Republican!
Long live America!
It was by you it first began.

LIBERTY'S BEACON.

What towering beacon light is this
   That points an Eagle starry sky?
Tis the Flag, the Flag, impress a kiss!
   Long may it wave its banners high!

Liberty—gleaming in the soul
   Will rise assert its mandate power;
Its triple thunders grasp the goal,
   Will calm each threatening lurid hour.

Ah! brightest, fondest, noblest page
   Whose altars lure a heavenly sky,
Our gallant sons through every age
   Will consecrate its temples high.

Tis Freedom! Stars and Stripes unite,
   The reflex of our Country's all;
And ever may their trident light
   Unnerve the arms who seek their fall.

It might reasonably be expected that in so large a mass of manuscript, sent in from so numerous and such widely separated places, there would be a plentiful sprinkling of those forms of bad English which have been christened Americanisms, in the spirit of the London shopkeeper who, as Boswell tells us, supposed the Earl of Marchmont, a highly educated Scotch nobleman, to be an American, "because, sir," said he, "you speak neither English nor Scotch, but something different from both, which I conclude is the language of America." But I have been able to discover only the following instance among all the manuscripts which have come into my hands.

> The land that invites all the oppressd. of the earth
>   To its bossom so open and free,
> My country ; I love thee ; no *human* can tell
>   The love that I bear unto thee.

But the following stanza from another hymn is of interest as containing an entirely new contribution to the "American" language. The author directs no special attention to it; but uses it quite in a matter of course way.

> Then let us hand in hand,
> Join in this Noble Band,
> The Whole of our Nation in *unionity* Join,
>   to stand by the union,
>   and old constitution till
> The last of the treators be Glad to give in.

Of quite a different cast from the songs that we have just been considering are the following homely verses; which might be called rude, were it not that their tenderness of sentiment is matched with a certain simple charm of language and sweetness of rhythm. The author, whom I conjecture to be a private soldier, stationed at one of our Western forts, writes, with frankness and modesty, "Please correct this if you think it is worth printing. I am no scholar." He is not indeed: he does not even know how to spell, and does not always rhyme; but I venture to say that he adds to a warm, true heart a genuine poetic temperament. His request I have complied with gladly; but only, it will be seen, as to orthography; and I do not envy any man who can read his crude and artless verses without emotion.

THE AMERICAN FLAG, OR BANNER.

            Unfurl your banners, let them fly,
            And wave in triumph to the sky!
            O'er the ocean, o'er the sea,
            O'er the land of liberty;
Chorus. O'er the land that God hath made
            For the gentle and the brave.

            O'er a land oppressed with strife,
            And o'er a nation dear as life:
            O'er a people deep in love
            With their country and their God.

            O'er a mother's heart that mourns
            For her country and her wrongs:
            O'er a father's heart so brave,
            Gently let it ever wave.

            O'er a sister's gentle love,
            And o'er a brother's, true and brave:
            O'er a wife so kind and true,
            And o'er the ocean, deep and blue.

            O'er the home that God hath bless'd,
            And o'er the land of heavenly peace:
            O'er our children let it wave
            When we are slumbering in our grave.

Of origin and appearance quite as unpromising as its predecessor, is the following significant composition; to be deterred from reading which by its bald rusticity will be to neglect a most characteristic national production; one which could have come out of no other country than our own, and from no other than a man of English race, who had been reared in the American Republic.

UNITED STATES NATIONAL HYMN, L. M.

Tune—*Yarmouth.*

BY JONATHAN —— ——

I.

God bless United States; each one
Has government, the people's own,
The people rule, their rulers are
Elected servants, to take care
Of what is for the public good;
And the best men, be chosen should;
And often changed, that surely we
May prosper, and be ever free.

II.

Foundation of our Union, find
On education, talent, mind;
God's Book, religion's only guide;
The supreme law, in all, reside;
Nor can majority oppress
Minority, but all confess
That each has Rights, which all must see
Respected in their purity.

III.

The Union, and the Nation, stand
A Government, o'er all the land;
Best, freest, strongest, wisest one,
Was, is, will be, beneath the sun;
The greatest numbers' greatest good;
And all protected, as we should;
Intelligence, ability,
For rulers, the best quality.

IV.

Jehovah, is our Head, and we
Acknowledge His supremacy;
He blesses us, year after year,
With all good things which do appear;
He is our Sovereign, only **one**
We'll have none else, till Time is done;
Three times a year acknowledge Him:
Fast, July Fourth, Thanksgiving time.

V.

As we march down the stream of Time,
New States, extend our happy clime;
Go on, increasing, good, and great;
One Union, formed of many States;
More States, the stronger, shall we be,
In union, peace, and liberty;
East, West, North, South, on sea and land,
Forever one, united stand.

VI.

Be every part, to each, most dear;
And law and order rule us here;
Our Constitutions, good and great,
Amended for the good of State;
Our statutes, for the people's good;
And Science guide us, as it should;
States within State; blest freedom's land,
United States forever stand!

VII.

Stand in thy strong integrity,
The North and South united be
With East and West, join heart and hand,
By our good Union firm to stand.

Our President, **elected be,**
By people's voice, **plurality;**
And the Vice-President the same;
The **highest offices of fame.**

VIII.

Free governments o'er earth will go;
The Bible, education too;
The righteous wise, shine as the sun;
Knowledge and Arts, o'er earth to run;
All know the Lord, His service be
Extended over land and sea;
His kingdom come, o'er men to reign,
And earth be all the Lord's. Amen.

JONATHAN —— ——

This hymn is dated from one of the remotest and most primitive of the rural districts of northern New England; and its chirography betrays a hand used to the plough and the hoe, not to the pen. The writer is plainly in a condition in life which in any other country would limit his knowledge to the delving of the few acres on which he lived. But rustic and unlettered as he is, what knowledge and intelligent comprehension his verses exhibit of the structure and the main principles of our government! How many statesmen and journalists abroad, undertaking to enlighten their colleagues or their readers on American affairs, do not speak five minutes, or write five sentences, without committing blunders which this unpretending rustic would at once discover and correct. Nor is his "hymn" or himself at all peculiar in this. Many of those received from various similar quarters showed a like knowledge and apprehension;

each one of these, too, being the production of a man who in this regard was but one of hundreds and thousands of his neighbors. For we must remember that thought and knowledge are not to be measured by the power to put them into rhyme. True, these men are better farmers and blacksmiths than poets. But there is need that they should be. Said Prince Napoleon, when he was told that a Lieutenant-Colonel, whom he saw at one of our volunteer camps, had been an *epicier*, "I cannot but see that a French Lieutenant-Colonel would be a better officer; but what I most think of is, how different a *man* in France the *epicier* would be."

The writer of this "Hymn," if he be not himself a type of the men who have made this country what it is, where slavery has not blighted it, has embodied in his verses the spirit and the principles which have animated those men, the very rudest and humblest of them, and enabled them to build up in the wilderness States, independent, self-sustaining, with as intelligent a purpose as that which they brought to the reclaiming of their fields and the raising of their log-houses. A statesman or a publicist trained in the schools and practised in politics, would set forth his theory of a state in which the best ends of government should be attained in language very different from that of this rustic hymn-writer. But, is there one, even among the best and wisest, who would not be obliged to confess that he could neither add to nor take from the plan in any important point? We are so familiar with this knowledge and with its diffusion that we take its presence **in any quarter and** under all circumstances as a matter of course. But if we will think of it we shall see that in the comprehensiveness and exactness of its setting forth of the essential features of our governmental structure, this **is a very** remarkable production. The reader has smiled at the quaint rudeness of the verses; but if he should read them again, I am in error if he **do not** smile also in a kind of admiration at the dexterity with which the writer has worked sound political and moral truth into them. Such men as this are worth more to a nation than colonels and poets. Such compositions, coming from such men, though falling short, or shooting wide of a national hymn, show that there is an unuttered hymn ever sounding in the breast of this nation, to embody which would **task the powers** of the mightiest poet that has ever sung.

VIII.

With the hymns sent to the committee, and after them, came many communications, some of a few lines and others of pages in length. With exceedingly rare exceptions, however, they were of interest only to the writers. Of those exceptions the following letter from "a lone female" is one of the most noticeable. It will be observed that publication is not only permitted but enjoined by the writer. I have, however, taken the liberty of suppressing her name and address. The letter has little to do with national hymns; but it is a most characteristic production. It is a genuine handful of the soil whence sprout Bloomers and Woman's Rights Conventions.

—— CONN., *May*, 1861.

Maunsell B Field and others of the National Hymn Committee New York City God the Father and Creator of all things has Caused Me to See a Notice in the N York Tribune that you are a , Committee to award a prize of Five Hundred dollars for a National Hymn.,,

The five hundred **dollars is a** great inducement to those that God has given that Talent. The knowledge that God has Created in *me* is to know how to accomplish the Mission **of the Saviour and bring** Peace on Earth and Good will amongst *Men* And the Committee knows that woman was Created for a help meet for *man*. And woman does help *Man* Create the family of *Man*. But in this Nation woman is Not allowed to help make Laws to Govern what she helps Create. And the Nation Cannot be Governed by righteous Laws without the knowledge of women to help make righteous Laws. And I want to ask the Committee what is the use of a National Hymn? where is it to be sung? is it to be sung in the Churches or is it to be sung when Men are going to Murder (war) and Make widows, and orphans, and wretchedness, **suffering** and *Death ?* And amongst the Names of the Committee are some **Noted** great Men in the State of New York the names of Gulian C Verplank, Charles King, Hamilton Fish, John A Dix, M. H. Grinnell and Luther Bradish I recognise as prominent Men in the political world but I do not recognise them as womans rights *Men* But I now appeal to them to organise a Committee to Call a Convention in N York City to Devise Means to Save Gods Creatures from the Devises and Cruelties of Satan And woman Must take equal rights in the Convention for woman is equal with *Man* in Creating the Family of *Man* And woman is not Inferior to Man in knowing what is right and wrong and the Committee knows that Murder (war) is wrong and the Committee knows that Ignominious Bondage (Slavery) is wrong and there is other Devices of Satan that is wrong and they are too Numerous to Mention on this sheet of Paper And if the Committee will call a Convention in the City of New York and extend the call to *women* to attend they will then *See* there is a work for woman to do to Save Life and Sinners in this Life that God the Saviour May save them in the Life to come The Committee knows that this Nation is frequently calld Uncle Sam,s Dominion and Men have Yet to learn that Uncle Sam,s Son,s are Not superior to Uncle Sam,s Daughters in either knowledge or Goodness And the Goodness of God must Descend through Uncle Sam,s Daughters so that the Blessing of God can come on all kindreds and Families of this *Earth* And as long as this Nation is Governed without the knowledge of *woman* this Nation Cannot become a United States and there will be Crimes poverty wretchedness and Deaths Caused by Murder (war) and other Devices of *Satan* And the Time has arrived that there Must be a Peaceable Revolution that will cause a Peaceable Reformation and have a *Peaceable Religion* organisd and have the Saviour,s (Mother) Church reorganised that must bend the Strong *Man* (satan) and destroy his works And the National hymn Committee Must disband and reorganise for a womans rights Committee and select one out of Uncle Sam,s Daughters to Govern this Nation there are Many Names that would not disgrace this Nation there is Lucretia Mott and Susan B Anthony and Elizabeth Cady Stanton and Ernestine L Rose and others too Numerous to Mention that are Not Inferior to their Siste-*Victoria* in either knowledge or Goodness And in this Nation when the subject of womans rights are to be discussed then woman is ridiculed and denounced as *Man,s* Inferior and there are but few that dare proclaim Gods Truths and say that woman is not Inferior to *Man* And if the National hymn Committee knows any thing about Gods Truths they know that *woman* eat of the Tree of knowledge as well as *Man* And that must teach the Committee and other Great Men of this Nation that the true knowledge of God Must come through the agency of *woman* as well as *Man*

And as soon as the National hymn Committee reorganise,s in a womans rights Committee then they can call a womans rights Convention and the objects of the Convention must be to Devise Means to establish Peace on Earth and Good will amongst Men And all Good and Great Men Must greatly desire to *See* that Great event so that Men will beat their swords Into plowshares and there spears Into pruning hooks and learn (Murder) war no

7

more and live in Peace and harmony with all *Men* And as the ,, hymn Committee ,, published ,, The request of many Citizens,, they must now publish the request of a lone Female that is striving to accomplish the Mission of the Saviour and save Gods Creatures in this Life from the Devises and Cruelties of Satan And I now subscribe My Name J**** C**** of Conn a Friend of Gods suffering Creatures J C.

The committee did not feel authorised to comply with the request of this "lone female," though they sincerely wished that her woes might be mitigated by the alleviation of her solitude. Not, however, to enter here into discussion of the question which the fair writer's letter brings up, I will tell her why one, at least, of the committee is not what she calls a woman's rights man. It is that, with all respect, honor, and tenderness for the sex, he believes that it is in all its characteristic traits and manifestations so different from the other, that the question of inferiority or superiority, nay even of equality, cannot be mooted between them more reasonably than whether a square is rounder than a circle, or as round;—that when the circle is squared then, and not before, will be settled the question of the relative importance of the functions of man and woman to the race;—and that among the peculiar functions of man is the administration of the world's affairs, because woman, with all her manifold virtues, her loveliness, her truth, her bright intelligence, her absolute self-devotion to those whom she loves—and whom if she did not thus love and give herself up to, the world would become a hideous waste of horror, and to none more so than to

her—yet has, has always had, and in the very nature
of things must ever have, such an incapacity to apprehend the fundamental laws of society and to comprehend and apply the principles of universal equity,
yes even of morality, such an inability to guide herself
by the rules of right reason, that if the control of affairs
should pass into her hands, the world would rush headlong into barbarism in a single generation,—that catastrophe against which she now opposes such a mighty
barrier. Were woman placed in power, absolute justice
would soon be lost sight of, and the law of the strongest
and the cunningest prevail. A woman despises the
very laws of nature when they interfere with the present
well-being of the man or the child she loves, and
would defy them if she could. As it is, at such times
she sits and eats her heart in anguish that she cannot
turn back the world upon its axis and stay the stars
in their courses; feeling the while that it is a personal
injustice that she is too weak to undertake those tasks.
This is right. The work she has to do is to see that
those she loves are made happy, quite regardless (in a
general way) of the manner and the reason of her
doing it; and just in so far as she accomplishes this,
and according to a high standard of happiness, does
she best serve mankind, vindicate her claim to an
equality with man, and maintain her blessed influence
over him. But this influence is vastly less than that
which he exercises over her. He is morally responsible for her; for she is always morally, almost mentally, just what he would have her be. This is the
law of her nature; the only law which in her inmost

soul she really respects; and even that respect she will not own. She stands breast-high to man; and all her thought cannot add a cubit to her stature.

The letters of few of the competitors were as interesting as Miss J. C.'s; but not a few of them were amusing exhibitions of the confident expectations of their writers. Some were accompanied with curt and clear directions as to where a check for Five Hundred Dollars might be sent. Others were in the following style. With a song beginning

"Our banner, our banner, long may it wave o'er us!
And the bird of our freedom long fly on before us!"

came the frank admission, "As I cannot conceive anything more suitable than the above, please send along the rocks, I have no use for medals." Another modestly adds at the bottom of a song much of the same quality, "I should prefer a medal to the money." Another sends an effusion of which the following is the first stanza:—

NATIONAL HYMN.

Great land of Freemen, brave and true!
The land that's left to me and you—
All nations seek thy sacred shore—
The "wished-for" shore in days of yore.
The precious blood of fathers slain
Was treasured in the earth like rain
And brought forth fruit;—and lo! we see
And taste—and feel and *know* we're free.

and winds up with this announcement, "N. B. Prize or no prize, I am not ashamed of these lines." But the wit of all these gentlemen was not concentrated within such brevity. They expatiated upon the beauties of their bantlings, and skilfully managed to work in a general puff of themselves—as for instance:—

—"The words and music are both by me, and I think that according to esthetics they are equal, even if not superior to my other works, which have attained the most brilliant success. I might improve it should you award me the prize, as every author can even in the case of his finest works. The music is perhaps better than the words. It is bold and grand, somewhat in the style of "God Save the king," although, as you will see, nothing like it."

The committee did see that it was not at all like "God Save the King." Comparison, however, they were not always called upon to make. Some competitors spoke in the positive mood. *Ecce Signum.*

The "——" is a splendid production in rhyme—measure—sentament—and rounded numbers—with an instructive national moral —the plot is well laid—revised corrected and polished by thought and reflection———Just such as the nation needs at this time— simple and easy of utterans—sings well and is liked by the ladys—it has been tryed by an organest and pronounced tiptop —The tune is not to be dispised for its name it will swell out like majestic thunder through the keys of an organ and move the heart of devotion by its melody—The committee should secure all of the rite to publish all of the hymns they would be quite a treet to conosiers of the music art! publish them all Pray do Pray do.

The reader of the foregoing pages does not need to

be told why this request, which was made with equal earnestness on all sides, is not complied with; and he may think that even the limited selection which has been made from the productions of the class which the petitioner represents might well have been abbreviated; while there are probably at least a thousand people in the land each one of whom has a profound conviction that a previous section of our libel* might have been well increased by the addition of one song, which shall be nameless. The opinion is perhaps natural; it is at least pardonable; and in some instances it may possibly be correct. Each competitor who has looked in vain through this booklet for that song which a circle of admiring, but strictly impartial, nay, look you, rather envious, friends had deemed surely worthy of the prize—good at sight for two hundred and fifty, if not five hundred dollars—to say nothing of the opinion of a certain person of fine natural taste and abilities, whose reputation is not quite so high as it deserves to be, and who had so often scrutinised it, without the slightest prejudice, and had yet been led to the same conclusion—every such competitor has an undeniable right to believe that that is the much-needed song, which by some oversight, or through the dulness of the committee, was ruthlessly basketed, and would have been irretreviably lost to the world, were it not for the wise precaution to which that carefully preserved

---

* *Libellus*, a little book. The word is used, of course, only in that sense.

and oft perused copy (which luckily can yet be found) was due. The others, of course, only met the fate which their writers, if they had possessed the least spark of modesty or self appreciation, might have expected for them. Because a national song is the product of peculiar circumstances, and—dont you see?—of peculiar qualifications,—not necessarily great, mind you, but peculiar; and is not something to be written by anybody and everybody, and to be made up of a certain number of rhyming lines about waving banners and spread eagles,—and with a mercenary motive too. It must come warm from the heart as that one did; and it must speak directly to the heart of the people as that one would speak, were it only allowed to be heard; and it must embody great sentiments common to the whole nation in strong and simple language as that one did—simple, you know, because that one was written by a person who don't make pretensions to be literary, whatever he *might* do; and such a song would have been sure to get the prize if there were any taste or any justice in the world.

O incensed competitor, you are right. Such a song as that would surely have taken the prize, if it had been found among the twelve hundred. That the song you wot of was awarded neither the five hundred dollars, nor a place where you sought it, must be because either it was not such a song, or the committee to whom it was voluntarily submitted had not the ability to perceive that it was. In either of which cases—don't you see?—you have no right to complain at all about the matter. And as to anything that has been said in this dissertation upon the subject of national hymns in general, or any hymn in particular, your capacity to write a national hymn will best appear by your preservation of a discreet silence. For there is not a cap between these covers that, except it is already labelled, the world will know fits you, unless you publicly put it on.

www.ingramcontent.com/pod-product-compliance
Lightning Source LLC
Chambersburg PA
CBHW030345170426
43202CB00010B/1253